THE MEMORY OF ABRAHAM LINCOLN
IS ENSHRINED FOREVER

American
Holidays

*Other Pro Lingua Books
about America:*

Plays for the Holidays
All Around America
Celebrating American Heroes
Heroes from American History
Legends
Living in the United States
North American Indian Tales

American Holidays

Exploring Traditions, Customs, and Backgrounds

Second, Revised Edition

Barbara Klebanow
Sara Fischer, Ph.D.

with illustrations by Robert MacLean

PRO LINGUA ASSOCIATES

Pro Lingua Associates, Publishers

P.O. Box 1348, Brattleboro, Vermont 05302 USA
Office: 802 257 7779 • Orders: 800 366 4775
E-mail: info@ProLinguaAssociates.com
WebStore www.ProLinguaAssociates.com
SAN: 216-0579

*At Pro Lingua
our objective is to foster an approach
to learning and teaching that we call
interplay, the **inter**action of language
learners and teachers with their materials,
with the language and culture,
and with each other in active, creative
and productive **play.***

Copyright © 1986, 2005 by Barbara Klebanow and Sara Fischer

ISBN 0-86647-196-0

This book was designed and set by Arthur A. Burrows and printed and bound by Capital City Press in Montpelier, Vermont. The subject of the book suggested the use of Palatino, a popular but traditional type much used by American typographers. The most widely used, and pirated, face of the twentieth century, Palatino was designed in Frankfurt in 1948 by Hermann Zapf. Although modern, it is based on Renaissance designs typical of the Palatinate area in Germany. Printing styles and technology have changed, but this elegant, easy-to-read type face has remained an American favorite into the digital age.

The drawings in this book are by Vermont artist Robert MacLean. The clipart and photographs illustrating the book are from *The Big Box of Art,* Copyright © 2001 Hemera Technologies Inc., *Art Explosion 750,000 Images,* Copyright © 1995-2000 Nova Development Corporation, and the wonderful Google Images Archive. Map of NY Harbor, U.S. Park Service. Photo p. xii Odessa College Veterans' Club website. Times Square photo p. 8 and Chinese New Year NYC p. 129 thanks to Annie M.G. Scmidt (beleven.org) in Amsterdam. Portraits of Dr. King on p. 14 from AP and on p. 16 © the Nobel Foundation, with permission. Celtic Pipers p. 40 from website of Downtown Milwaukee's 2005 St. Patrick's Day Parade. Easter basket p. 44 AwesomeClipartforKids.com; bunny p. 44 Coloringbookfun.com. Mother's and Father's Day photo, credit U.S. Census Bureau. Memorial Day parade, p. 60, vfwpost672.0rd/days_gone_by.html. 4 July photos p. 63: Dave 7/4/2003 astro,psu.edu; 3 kids, Skylar Pictures; parade with bike, Hyde Park, Chicago. 4 July photos p. 64: Buckaroo Float, clownsofdeath.com/pix Bear Valley Springs. Thanksgiving p.10 credit LovingYou. Children's Chinese New Year party p. 129, thanks to the Cottage School, Sharon, Mass. Cinco de Mayo parades in San Jose, Cal., by Andreas Dieberger. Sgt. Myers' Kwanzaa thanks to Hanscomb AFB. Clowning with Chinese NY Dragon in Chicago p. 137, credit John Ng. Christmas pageant p.138 credit Northampton Pres. Church. Yom Kippur p. 142 credit Ohr HaTorah, LA, CA. Cadet D. Wallace p. 164 thanks to U.S. Dept. of State Bureau of Information Program. Front cover photo of Boston fireworks © by AP/WWP Adam Hunger, July 4th, 2002. Back cover photo of Scouts, *Art Explosion 750,000 Images.*

Printed in the United States of America.
Second, revised edition. Second Printing 2012. 31,000 copies in print.

Acknowledgements

Thanks to my parents, Manya and Barnett Brodie, who fled their homeland seeking economic and religious freedom as well as a land of opportunity for their children – my brother was able to become a medical doctor and I, a teacher. Teaching students from different countries in the Great Neck public schools and the North Shore Hospital in Manhasset, I have learned again and again of the sacrifices people make leaving their homeland and all their dear ones; my students demonstrated great strength and courage. It was these qualities that inspired me to to write this book in hope that it would help them achieve their goals and feel comfortable with the customs and traditions of America, their new home. My husband Isidore has been a wonderful helpmate as we enjoy our four children and nine grandchildren together. —*Barbara Klebanow*

In the 19 years since this book was first published, my love and dedication to learning and teaching have continued to grow. In the past 30 years I have met dozens of dedicated teachers and hundreds of eager students who have reinforced the notion that education is the key to a good life, a life of spiritual and educational growth. Language is the main avenue we humans use to communicate, and helping people improve their English so that they can more easily traverse the culture and the environment of this country fills me with awe and satisfaction.

As in the first edition, I want to thank again my children Albert, Fabiana, and Alexandra Lotito for their love and support. But now, I also need to add a word of thanks to my grandchildren Tiana, Michelle, Justin, Rebecca, and Gavin. Their existence points the way to a brighter future and to a place filled with learning, excitement, and kind love. They constantly offer me new opportunities to observe closely how we learn and experience the world. I cannot imagine my life without them. I love them dearly.

Special thanks to my friend Rosemarie Ferrara for her wise counsel and support. — *Dr. Sara Fischer*

Special thanks are due to the Great Neck Public Library whose resources were always extended to us most graciously. The New York Times also proved to be a helpful resource. — *BK and SF*

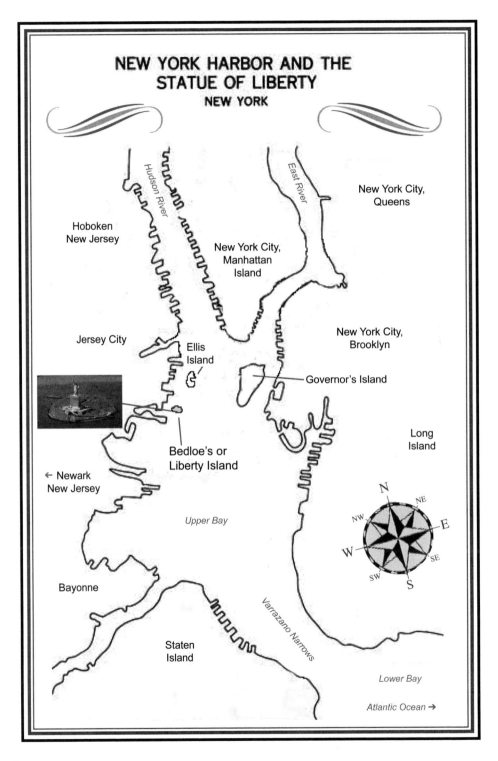

NEW YORK HARBOR AND THE
STATUE OF LIBERTY
NEW YORK

Hudson River

East River

New York City,
Queens

Hoboken
New Jersey

New York City,
Manhattan
Island

Jersey City

Ellis
Island

New York City,
Brooklyn

Governor's Island

Bedloe's or
Liberty Island

Long
Island

← Newark
New Jersey

Upper Bay

N
NE
NW
E
W
SE
SW
S

Bayonne

Varrazano Narrows

Staten
Island

Lower Bay

Atlantic Ocean →

I dedicate this book to Liberty's greatest symbol,

The Statue of Liberty.

– Barbara Klebanow

Give me your tired, your poor,
Your huddled masses yearning to breathe free,
The wretched refuse of your teeming shore.
Send these, the homeless, tempest-tost to me,
I lift my lamp beside the golden door!

from *The New Colossus*
by Emma Lazarus

Traditional flowers for the holidays.
Easter lilies are a favorite at Easter,
and bright red pointsettas decorate homes and
public places for Christmas.

Contents

Introduction for the student and teacher   xv

1. Introductory Reading   1

__ legal
__ religious

__ celebrate
__ superstition

__ commemorate
__ calendar

2. New Year's Day   7

__ ancient
__ prosperity
__ float
__ resolution

__ embrace
__ crowd
__ goal

__ toast
__ elaborate
__ achieve

3. Martin Luther King, Jr.'s Birthday   14

__ rights
__ integrate
__ memorial
__ assassin

__ racial
__ injustice
__ spiritual

__ discrimination
__ segregate
__ clergyman

4. Valentine's Day   21

__ festival
__ sweetheart
__ merchant
__ feelings

__ romance
__ humorous
__ decorate

__ affection
__ companion
__ spouse

Contents

5. Presidents' Day   29

__ portrait
__ independence
__ refuse
__ ideal

__ admit
__ elect
__ conflict

__ wrongdoing
__ unanimously
__ unite

6. St. Patrick's Day   37

__ descent
__ participate
__ capture
__ legend

__ celebrity
__ pennant
__ convert

__ bystanders
__ estimate
__ miracle

7. Easter   44

__ coincide
__ symbol
__ gift
__ rebirth

__ renewal
__ greeting card
__ dyed

__ yearly
__ basket
__ parade

8. Mother's Day and Father's Day   51

__ respect
__ role
__ value
__ establish

__ raise
__ get together
__ thoughts

__ opportunity
__ memories
__ proclaim

9. Memorial Day   57

__ patriotic
__ grave
__ origin
__ needy

__ disabled
__ cemetery
__ tragedy

__ service
__ veterans
__ benefit

10. Independence Day • The 4th of July 63

__ declare   __ free   __ organize
__ perform   __ naturalization   __ swear in
__ representation   __ force   __ obey
__ recognize

11. Labor Day 71

__ union   __ message   __ hire
__ wages   __ persuade   __ require
__ minimum   __ strike   __ competition
__ solution

12. Columbus Day 78

__ contribution   __ tie   __ route
__ convince   __ finance   __ expedition
__ comfort   __ crude   __ navigate
__ encourage

13. Halloween 86

__ holy   __ costumes   __ ghost
__ character   __ trick   __ treat
__ collect   __ carve   __ scary
__ evil

14. Election Day 92

__ election   __ vote   __ registration
__ advertise   __ privacy   __ candidate
__ result   __ campaign   __ duty
__ debate

*Veterans during the 2003 Veterans Day flag raising ceremony
at Odessa College in Texas*

15. Veterans Day 99

___ remember   ___ honor   ___ missing
___ courage   ___ observe   ___ ceremony
___ monument   ___ bury   ___ enact
___ dedicated

16. Thanksgiving Day 106

___ faiths   ___ blessing   ___ feast
___ annual   ___ balloon   ___ wreath
___ elderly   ___ starvation   ___ survive
___ harvest

17. Christmas 114

___ share   ___ exchange   ___ sparkle
___ display   ___ ornaments   ___ present
___ favorite   ___ donation   ___ volunteer
___ vacation

18. Birthdays   121

__ invitation   __ candle   __ wishes
__ traditional   __ appropriate   __ souvenir
__ catered   __ reserve   __ refreshments
__ charities

19. Cultural Holidays   128

Chinese New Year   128

Cinco de Mayo   130

Kwanzaa   131

__ lunar   __ farewell   __ reward
__ defend   __ twice   __ heritage
__ pride   __ ancestor   __ focus
__ creativity

20. Religious Holidays   138

CHRISTIAN HOLIDAYS • Christmas, Easter   138

MUSLIM HOLIDAYS • Ramadan, Id-al-Fitr, Id-al-Adha   140

JEWISH HOLIDAYS • Rosh Hashanah & Yom Kippur,

Passover & Hanukkah   142

__ major   __ anniversary   __ fast
__ dawn   __ prayer   __ gather
__ occur   __ repentance   __ get rid of
__ atone

Appendices   149

   Readings for the Holidays   150

   Songs for the Holidays   158

   Some State Holidays   160

   Gifts for Holidays and Other Occasions   162

Answers   164

Suggestions for the Teacher   169

   For Self-Study   169

   For Group Study   169

   General Suggestions   171

Key Word Index   173

Introduction
for the student and teacher

American Holidays is a vocabulary development text which focuses on words which are associated with the traditions, customs, and background of the special days we celebrate in the United States. Some of these holidays are also celebrated in Canada and elsewhere. The key vocabulary is presented in twenty readings. The reading passages are written in a redundant style so that you can understand each key word by looking at its context. In other words, you should try to understand the meaning of the word by studying the words and sentences which precede and follow the key word. Of course, you may want to use a dictionary from time to time. In this way you can develop both new vocabulary and good reading skills. The lessons are organized according to the following plan:

Reading

Each reading selection describes an American holiday. The key vocabulary is in **boldface**. The first section of each reading explains the traditions and customs of the holiday. The second explores its historical and cultural background.

Exercises

Several exercises follow each reading selection. The exercises progress from easy to more difficult. In the exercises you will be required to explore the forms and meanings of the key words.

The exercises are not tests. They are teaching exercises, and it is expected that you will make some mistakes. You can teach yourself by using the answers in the back of the book. The next-to-last exercise does not have answers in the book because you must create original sentences. You can use this exercise as a test by asking someone who knows English well to check your answers.

Internet Search

Finally, you will see some web sites that have more information about the holiday. If you have access to the Internet, check out these sites.

Appendices

Each appendix contains materials chosen to supplement the readings and exercises on the holidays. There are readings of historical importance and songs sung or at least often heard on certain holidays. A list of state and other holidays and a reading on gift giving at holidays and other times have been appended as well.

Answers

Answers for most of the exercises are at the back of the book.

Suggestions for the Teacher

Basic techniques for using this book and ideas for supplementing it are described in this section.

Key Word Index

This is a list of all the key words and the lessons in which they appear.

Introductory Reading

🎃	**20____**	💘	
January ☆ ☆	February ☆ ☆	March ☆	April
May ☆ ☆	June	July ☆	August
September ☆	October ☆ ☆	November ☆ ☆ ☆	December ☆

There are many special days in the United States; some of them are **legal** holidays. On a legal holiday, schools, businesses, and government offices are usually closed. Legal holidays are also called federal holidays because all federal government offices are closed. Many people do not go to work. There are ten legal holidays that are observed throughout the country.

Some states **celebrate** local holidays to **commemorate** events that are important to that state or region. They remember and honor important local events. For example, on or about April 19, a famous date of the American Revolution, Massachusetts and Maine celebrate Patriots' Day. On this day, the famous race, the Boston Marathon, is held.

There are also several special **religious** days. The word "holiday" is a combination of "holy" and "day," but the only religious day that is also a legal holiday is Christmas. Other well known religious days are Good Friday and Easter (Christian), Rosh Hashanah and Yom Kippur (Jewish), and Id-al-Fitr and Id-al-Adha (Muslim).

There are also special days that are not holidays or commemorative days. One of these days is February 2nd, when people in the northern part of the United States are beginning to look forward to spring. It is called Groundhog Day. There is a **superstition** that on this day a small animal, the groundhog, comes out of its hole in the ground where it has spent the winter. If the sun is shining and it sees its shadow, it will go back in its hole and there will be six more weeks of winter. If the sun is not shining, the groundhog will stay out and spring will come early.

April Fools' Day is the first day of April, a time when spring is coming and people are feeling playful. On this day people play tricks on each other. A favorite trick is to say something that is not true. If another person believes what is said, they are an "April Fool."

From time to time, Friday comes on the 13th day of the month. Friday the Thirteenth is considered an unlucky day, and some superstitious people are very careful because they are afraid that something bad may happen during the day.

The readings in this book describe the best known legal holidays and commemorative days. You can find most of them on your **calendar**. August is the only month in the calendar year that never has a holiday.

Now do the exercises and check your answers. If you can do the Internet search, fill in the dates of this year's holidays on page 6. If you cannot use the Internet, find the dates on a calendar.

Exercises (ANSWERS ON PAGE 164)

I. Use the words below to complete the sentences.

legal	celebrate	superstition
religious	commemorate	calendar

1. There are ten _____ holidays in the United States.
2. Groundhog Day is based on a _____.
3. Some states _____ their own holidays.
4. Easter is a _____ day.
5. There is a _____ on the wall.
6. Patriots' Day _____s the patriots of the American Revolution.

II. Use these forms of the key words to complete the sentences.

illegal	religion	commemorative
legally	celebration	superstitious

1. He is not scared of Friday the Thirteenth because he is

   not _____.

1999   *1979*

2. The government issued two _____ postage stamps for Martin Luther King, Jr.

3. It is _____ to drink alcohol and drive a car at the same time.

4. In 1986 there was a great _____ for the Statue of Liberty.

5. A person without a driver's license cannot _____ drive a car.

6. Christianity is not the official _____ of the United States.

III. Respond to these statements and questions with a sentence

1. Name one religious holiday.

   _____

2. What does Patriots' Day commemorate?

   _____

3. How many calendars do you have?

   _____

4. Do you celebrate any religious holidays?

   _____

5. When is the next legal holiday?

   _____

6. Do you have any superstitions?

   _____

IV. Search the Internet to find out more about holidays in the US. You can begin by checking this site: www.holidays.net. Click on <u>Days and Dates</u>. Then fill in the list of holidays for this year.

Holidays for 20___	Month	Day	Date
New Year's Day			
Martin Luther King, Jr.'s Birthday			
Chinese New Year			
Valentine's Day			
Presidents' Day			
St. Patrick's Day			
Easter			
Cinco de Mayo			
Mother's Day			
Memorial Day			
Father's Day			
Independence Day			
Labor Day			
Columbus Day			
Halloween			
Veterans Day			
Election Day			
Thanksgiving			
Christmas			
Kwanzaa			
Id-il-Fitr			
Id-il-Adha			
Rosh Hashanah			
Yom Kippur			
Hanukkah			
Your birthday			

New Year's Day

January 1. 20__

1

_____ DAY

Traditions and Customs

New Year's Day is a legal holiday celebrated in the United States. The celebration begins on December 31, New Year's Eve, the night before New Year's Day. Many people stay up until midnight. Some go to church while others go to parties. Horns, whistles, and other noisemakers are very popular on this night. This is an old tradition from **ancient** times when people made loud noises to scare away evil spirits.

When the ringing of bells and the blowing of whistles and horns announce that the new year has started, some people shake hands; others kiss and **embrace**. Many join together to sing "Auld Lang Syne." In addition to blowing whistles and horns, people throw paper confetti and streamers and call out "Happy New Year," raising their drinks in a **toast** to the future, hoping it will bring health, peace, and **prosperity**.

In Times Square in New York City each New Year's Eve at midnight the ball falls and the party begins. Millions of people watch the party on TV.

On New Year's Eve, many cities have a celebration called "First Night." New York City holds an outdoor event which attracts a **crowd** of a million or more people. The event is televised around the country. A large ball shaped like an apple and covered with bright lights is slowly lowered from a pole on top of a tall building in Times Square. It starts coming down one minute before midnight. When it reaches the bottom of the pole, the new year has begun.

New Year's Day is celebrated in different ways. Many people hold "Open House," serving refreshments to visitors. Eggnog, a drink made with milk and eggs, is especially popular. Others watch the parades and football games that are typical of this day. The Mummers' Parade in Philadelphia has marchers in **elaborate** costumes. The Tournament of Roses parade in Pasadena, California, is known for its floats decorated with fresh flowers. The most famous college football game, the Rose Bowl, is played after the parade.

Background

New Year's Day celebrates the start of a new year. People who follow the Roman calendar celebrate this holiday on January first. This month was named for Janus, the ancient Roman god with two faces, one looking into the past, the other looking into the future.

On New Year's Day people often think about the past year. They remember the projects they finished and the **goals** they did not **achieve**. Like Janus, they also look forward to a new beginning and make "new year **resolutions**" on what they will achieve.

On New Year's Day families often watch the Tournament of Roses parade on TV.
There are many bands and floats in the parade. There are also many horses.
Here the Rita Ranch Cowboy Girls do rope tricks on horseback.

Photo by Galen R. Frysinger (www.galenfrysinger.com)

Exercises (ANSWERS ON PAGE 164)

I. Match each word with its meaning.

1. toast   _____ a. many people
2. achieve   _____ b. detailed; complicated
3. elaborate   _____ c. to do successfully
4. resolution   _____ d. decorated vehicle
5. goal   _____ e. very old
6. prosperity   _____ f. something to work for
7. embrace   _____ g. a firm decision
8. ancient   _____ h. an expression of affection; a hug
9. crowd   _____ i. good fortune; success
10. float   _____ j. a drink to honor someone or something

II. Choose the best word to complete each sentence.

1. Football games attract a large (crowd, parade, toast).

2. Some marchers in the parade wear (hats, toast, elaborate) costumes.

3. The (crowds, floats, people) in the "Tournament of Roses" parade are covered with fresh flowers.

4. Making loud noises on New Year's Eve is a tradition that began in (ancient, modern, cold) times.

5. We all hope to (toast, achieve, decorate) our goals in the coming year.

6. People should make (crowds, goals, prosperity) for the new year.

7. At midnight people kiss and (achieve, sit, embrace) one another.

8. Most people make (resolutions, parties, embraces) that are difficult to keep.

9. Everybody hopes that the new year brings (prosperity, tradition, goals) and health.

10. When the new year arrives, many people raise their glasses and make a (achieve, toast, resolve) to the future.

III. Complete the following passage.

   Everybody expects large _____ in Times Square on New Year's Eve. When the apple reaches the bottom of the pole, people shout "Happy New Year" and _____ one another. At the same time, people at parties blow whistles and horns, following an _____ tradition. They _____ with champagne and think about their _____ for the new year. They make _____ to improve their lives, and hope they can keep them. Everyone looks to the future for peace and _____. The following day, many families watch parades. They enjoy the _____ covered with flowers and the marchers in _____ costumes.

   IV. Complete these sentences.

   1. The wedding celebration started with a _____ to the newly married couple.

   2. The young couple worked hard so they could enjoy _____ in later years

   3. The Pyramids and the Sphinx are monuments of _____ Egypt.

   4. The athlete achieved her _____ when she won an Olympic gold medal.

   5. The oriental rug was decorated with an _____ design.

   6. The rock concert attracted a noisy _____.

   7. Musicians practice long hours to _____ their artistic goals.

   8. The old friends _____ with emotion after the long absence.

   9. The sisters promised to tell each other their New Year's _____.

   10. The students worked many hours to finish the _____ for the college parade.

V. Write questions that can be answered by each statement below.
The first word of each question has been written for you.

Example: People celebrate the new year with noisemakers.

   a. How *do people celebrate the new year*?

1. The New Year's holiday begins on the evening of December 31st.

   a. What _____?
   b. When _____?

2. Large crowds attend the outdoor event in Times Square, New York City.

   a. Who _____?
   b. Where _____?

3. Americans go to parties to celebrate the new year.

   a. Who _____?
   b. Where _____?
   c. Why _____?

4. Alfredo made a resolution during the New Year's holiday.

  a. Who _____?

  b. What _____?

  c. When _____?

5. In ancient times people made loud noises to scare away evil spirits.

  a. Who _____?

  b. What _____?

  c. Why _____?

VI. Use the Internet to learn more about New Year's Day.

  1. Find out more traditions related to the new year. Find out when people started to use a baby to symbolize a new year.

    http://wilstar.com/holidays/newyear.htm

  2. Research this site to find out about decorations for New Year's Day.

    http://www.homeandfamilynetwork.com/holidays/newyears.html

Martin Luther King, Jr.'s Birthday

January ___, 20___

———

MONDAY

Traditions and Customs

The third Monday in January is a legal holiday to honor Martin Luther King, Jr., who was born on January 15th. He was a great civil **rights** leader who fought against **racial discrimination**. He said that people should be judged by their character, and not the color of their skin. He believed in **integration**. He received national attention when he protested the **injustice** of **segregated** buses in Alabama.

Martin Luther King, Jr. is remembered in church **memorial** services, marches, and public ceremonies. People also listen to his speeches, watch TV documentaries, and sing **spirituals** and the civil rights anthem "We Shall Overcome."

In schools, students read about this leader, study his writings and celebrate his memory with special programs. Politicians and performers also participate in celebrations to honor Martin Luther King, Jr.

Background

Martin Luther King, Jr., was born in Atlanta, Georgia, on January 15th, 1929. His father was a **clergyman**, Reverend Martin Luther King, Sr., and his mother was Alberta Williams King.

Martin Luther King, Jr., was an excellent student. He entered college at the age of 15. He was interested in history, literature, sociology, and public speaking. He studied black history, religion, and theology. He received his doctor of philosophy degree from Boston University. He became a minister and married Coretta Scott. They had four children. He became the pastor of the Dexter Avenue Baptist Church in Montgomery, Alabama.

Dr. King was given the Nobel Peace Prize. This is the official Nobel portrait taken in 1964.

Martin Luther King, Jr., worked to end segregation of black people. He worked to give civil rights to everyone in the United States. In addition to his civil rights work, he also became a leader of the international human rights movement.

He believed in non-violent methods. In 1963, he gave one of his most famous speeches, "I Have a Dream," in front of the Lincoln Memorial, in Washington, D.C. That day he led a peace march of 250,000 people. They wanted to ensure the rights of the Constitution to all people in the United States.

He became famous and was loved and respected by many people all around the world. He received the Nobel Peace Prize in 1964. Martin Luther King, Jr. died at the age of 39 years. He was killed by an **assassin**. It was a very sad day for the American people and the world.

Exercises (Answers on page 164)

I. Match the words with similar meanings.

1. memorial	_____	a.	religious song
2. clergyman	_____	b.	killer
3. segregate	_____	c.	unfairness
4. rights	_____	d.	bringing groups of people together, combining
5. racial	_____	e.	remembrance; something done to remember or honor a person
6. injustice	_____	f.	being unfair to a group of people because of their color, religion, etc.
7. integration	_____	g.	separate
8. assassin	_____	h.	grouped by skin color, appearance, etc.
9. spiritual	_____	i.	privileges
10. discrimination	_____	j.	pastor; minister

II. Circle the word that will best complete each sentence.

1. Many people attend (justice, memorial) services in honor of Martin Luther King, Jr.

2. Martin Luther King, Jr. worked to end (segregation, ethnic) of black people; he believed that all men are equal.

3. He wanted people of all races to be (injustice, integrated).

4. Martin Luther King, Jr., worked to end (discrimination, rights) against black people.

5. A person who kills is called an (assassination, assassin).

6. The (memorial, spiritual) "We Shall Overcome" is recognized as the Civil Rights Anthem.

7. The church memorial service in honor of Martin Luther King, Jr. was conducted by a (spiritual, clergyman).

8. All people should believe that (racial, spiritual) differences are not important, but that all human beings have the same (segregation, rights).

9. People who fight for equality know that it is a(n) (segregation, injustice) to judge people by the color of their skin.

III. Select words to complete the sentences below.

1. Marian Anderson sang _____ and other songs in her concert.

2. It is an _____ to be punished for a crime you did not commit.

3. The _____ married four couples in one afternoon.

4. In the United States boys and girls are not _____ in public schools; they all are in the same class.

5. A large crowd attended the outdoor _____ service to remember and honor the heroes.

6. Men and women must have the same _____ since the Constitution guarantees equality for all.

7. Many different _____ groups can be found in New York City, since people from all over the world come to live in the United States.

8. It is against the law for employers to _____ against employees because of their nationality.

9. The police found the _____ and he was brought to trial.

10. Public schools cannot separate boys and girls in different classes; they all have to be _____.

IV. Complete these sentences.

1. The artist designed a monument to honor and remember the famous hero.
   He created a _____ .

2. On Martin Luther King, Jr.'s birthday, people sang "We Shall Overcome."
   They sang a _____.

3. "All men are created equal."
   This is a statement of _____ equality.

4. All youngsters from the age of 5 to 21 can go to public school.
   It is their _____ .

5. In the United States, students cannot be separated because of their race or religion. _____ is illegal.

V. Circle the word that does not belong.

1. clergyman   actor   minister   pastor

2. inequality   democracy   injustice   discrimination

3. separation   integration   combination   togetherness

4. killer   criminal   fireman   assassin

5. discrimination   unfairness   justice   inequality

VI. Write questions for each of these sentences. Ask about the word or phrase that is in italics.

Example: Jackie Robinson *played* baseball.
     What did Jackie Robinson do?

1. Muhammad Ali won many *boxing matches*.

_____?

2._Ralph Bunche_ was awarded the Nobel Peace Prize.

_____?

3. Langston Hughes wrote _hundreds_ of poems.

_____?

4. Colin Powell attended many _international_ conferences.

_____?

5. Oprah Winfrey _hosts_ a TV show.

_____?

6. _Shirley Chisholm_was the first black woman in the U.S. Congress.

_____?

7. Marian Anderson sang _at the Lincoln Memorial._

_____?

8. George Washington Carver was _a scientist._

_____?

9. _Duke Ellington's_ band played "Take the A Train."

_____?

10. Paul Robeson won many theatrical awards _because of his great acting._

_____?

VII. Use the Internet to find out more about Martin Luther King, Jr.

1. Find out how to plan a visit to the Martin Luther King Jr.'s Birth Home Museum.

   http://www.nps.gov/malu

2. Go to the Biography section and listen to some of Martin Luther King, Jr.'s speeches.

   http://seattletimes.nwsource.com/mlk

3. Read about the history of Martin Luther King, Jr.'s Day; write a report.

   http://www.infoplease.com/spot/mlkjrday1.html

Valentine's Day

February 14, 20__

14

____DAY

Traditions and Customs

Valentine's day is celebrated on February 14th as a **festival** of **romance** and **affection**. People send greeting cards called "valentines" to their **sweethearts**, friends, and members of their families.

Many valentines have romantic poems; others are **humorous**. But almost all valentines ask "Be My Valentine." This may mean be my friend or be my love or be my **companion**. Valentines often show a cupid with an arrow. Cupid, also called Eros, was the ancient Roman god of love.

Valentine's day is not a legal holiday; schools and banks are open as usual. **Merchants** sell valentines and **decorations** for Valentine's Day parties and dances. All the decorations are bright red, and the most popular ones are heart shaped. Stores advertise heavily for this holiday since it is traditional for sweethearts, **spouses**, and members of the family to exchange gifts on Valentine's Day. Heart-shaped boxes of candy, jewelry, and flowers are some of the popular gifts given on this day.

School children decorate their classrooms with bright red paper hearts and celebrate the day in their classroom. They also make valentine cards for their friends and parents.

Many newspapers carry advertisements or messages placed by people in love. Both men and women want to let their sweethearts know how much they love them. On Valentine's Day, many radio stations play romantic music all day long. One very famous song is called "My Funny Valentine."

Valentine's Day is a day to share loving **feelings** with friends and family. It has become traditional for many couples to become engaged on this day. Also, famous couples are remembered. Some of them are Romeo and Juliet, Caesar and Cleopatra, among others. This is a happy day because it is specially dedicated to celebrate love, affection, and friendship.

Background

Valentine's Day comes on the feast of two different Christian saints named Valentine. But the way that Valentine's Day is celebrated has nothing to do with the lives of the saints.

This celebration comes from an ancient Roman festival called "Lupercalia," which took place every February 15th. This festival honored Juno, the Roman goddess of women and marriage, and Pan, the god of nature. It was also believed that birds chose their mates on this date. Valentine's Day became very popular in the United States in the 1800's.

Exercises (ANSWERS ON PAGE 164)

I. Match words with similar meanings.

1. romance   _____ a. boyfriend; girlfriend
2. affection   _____ b. love
3. humorous   _____ c. tenderness; warm feelings
4. decorate   _____ d. make attractive
5. merchant   _____ e. wife or husband
6. spouse   _____ f. emotions
7 . feelings   _____ g. funny
8. companion   _____ h. celebration
9. festival   _____ i. storekeeper
10. sweetheart   _____ j. friend

II. Cross out the phrases or words that don't belong.

1. humorous >
   a. serious
   b. funny
   c. light-hearted
   d. comic

2. affection >
   a. a hug
   b. a kiss
   c. caring
   d. anger

3. merchant >
   a. customer
   b. salesperson
   c. seller
   d. florist

4. feelings >
   a. love
   b. anger
   c. homework
   d. happiness

5. companion >
   a. a person
   b. a friend
   c. a car
   d. a roommate

6. festival >
   a. a party
   b. a celebration
   c. a funeral
   d. a parade

7. sweetheart >
   a. boyfriend
   b. enemy
   c. wife
   d. husband

8. spouse >   a. husband
                             b. mate
                             c. parent
                             d. wife

9. decorations >   a. paper hearts
                             b. flowers
                             c. pictures
                             d. dresses

10. romance >   a. relationship
                             b. affair
                             c. love
                             d. fight

III. Select the word that best completes the sentence.

1. On the classroom walls there are (celebrations, decorations, festivals).

2. Valentine's Day is a celebration of love and (romance, decorations, parents).

3. Valentine cards have messages of (affection, humorous, share).

4. It is traditional to send flowers to (celebrate, spouses, dedicate) on Valentine's Day.

5. On this day people share feelings of affection with friends, family, and (flowers, affection, companions).

6. (Sweethearts, Spouses, Merchants) decorate their stores with red hearts and cupids on Valentine's day.

7. This is a day to celebrate (feelings, humorous, decorations) of friendship and love.

8. Some Valentine cards are funny; they have (loving, humorous, romance) messages.

9. Lupercalia was an ancient Roman (sharing, god, festival).

10. Many people call people they love (sweetheart, romance, spouse).

IV. Fill in the blanks with appropriate words.

1. Romeo and Juliet loved each other very much; but their parents didn't know it.
   They had a secret _____.

2. The young man got married.
   Now he has a _____.

3. Mary likes John very much.
   She has good _____ toward him.

4. The grandmother asked her grandchild to go with her on the trip to Washington.
   She asked her to be her traveling _____.

5. The village of River Falls celebrates spring every year.
   The event is called the River Falls Spring _____.

6. Martin told Helene: "I have warm feelings for you."
   He feels _____ for her.

7. Everybody laughed when they heard the story.
   It was very _____.

8. The couple was very much in love.
   They called each other _____.

9. The owners of the stores formed a group association.
   It is a group of _____.

V. Select the correct word form to complete each sentence.

1. It is a (romance, romantic) poem. It's about their wonderful (romance, romantic).

2. The spring party was a (festival, festive) occasion. It was a great (festival, festive).

3. The TV comedy was very (humor, humorous). It was full of good (humor, humorous).

4. The Christmas tree was (decorated, decorations) with colored lights. The (decorated, decorations) were mostly red.

5. He wrote about his (affection, affectionate) for her. He is very (affection, affectionate).

VI. Unscramble and rewrite these sentences.

Example: in love Juliet Romeo and were
_____ *Romeo and Juliet were in love.*

1. was Yoko Ono wife John Lennon's

   _____.

2. an apple Eve Adam gave

   _____.

3. the Monaco of Prince married Grace Kelly

_____.

　　　　　　　　or

_____.

4. Tarzan rescued was by Jane

_____.

5. taller was Josephine Napoleon than

_____.

6. Miss Piggy love in with is the frog Kermit

_____.

7. Elizabeth Taylor husbands had many

_____.

8. lovers Rhett Butler *Gone the Wind with* in were Scarlett O'Hara and

_____.

VII. Use the Internet to find out more about Valentine's Day.

1. Find out about the first written "valentines."

http://people.howstuffworks.com/valentine.htm

2. Read about the story of Cupid, the most famous of Valentine's Day symbols.

http://www.holidays.net/amore/cupid.html

3. Find out how Valentine's Day is celebrated in other parts of the world.

http://www.annieshomepage.com/valhistory.html

Presidents' Day

February __, 20__

_____

MONDAY

Traditions and Customs

In February, the United States honors two great American presidents: Abraham Lincoln, on February 12th, and George Washington, on February 22nd. These two days are combined into one legal holiday on the third Monday in February, called Presidents' Day.

Both presidents have been honored in different ways. George Washington is the only president to have a state named after him. The nation's capital, Washington, D.C., also has his name. There are cities, towns, streets, schools, bridges, and parks named after both President Lincoln and President Washington. Both have famous memorials in Washington, D.C. Their **portraits** also appear on postage stamps, bills, and coins. Washington's house in Mount Vernon and Lincoln's home in Springfield, Illinois, have been made into museums.

Cherry pie is a traditional food for Washington's Birthday because of a popular legend. It is said that as a boy Washington chopped down his father's cherry tree. When asked by his father, he **admitted** to his **wrongdoing** and said, 'I cannot tell a lie."

Background

George Washington, known as the "Father of His Country" was born on February 22nd, 1732, in Westmoreland County, Virginia.

Washington helped shape the beginning of the United States in three important ways. First, he was the commander in chief of the Continental Army that won **independence** for 13 British colonies from Great Britain in the Revolutionary War. Secondly, in 1787, Washington served as president of the Constitutional Convention that wrote the United States Constitution. Lastly, George Washington was the first **elected** president of the U.S. He was the only president to be elected **unanimously**. He served a second term of office and **refused** a third term. He died on December 14th, 1799, at Mount Vernon at the age of 67.

Lincoln was born on February 12th, 1809, in a log cabin in Kentucky. He was elected the 16th President of the United States. It is said that, if he had not lived, the United States might be two countries today, instead of one. Lincoln was president during a difficult period of American history. Just before he started his presidency, seven southern states broke away from the United States and started their own country.

They called it the Confederate States of America and elected their own president, Jefferson Davis. The country was divided and involved in a civil war. President Lincoln was able to end the **conflict** and **unite** the country.

Photography was a new art form during the Civil War. Some of the greatest photos were taken of the President. This was the last. It was taken just before his death, days after the end of the war.

President Lincoln is praised and remembered for his belief in democracy, in the equality of all men, and his fight for freedom for all. He believed slavery to be a cruel and evil practice. His famous speech "The Gettysburg Address" expresses his **ideals**. It has become a lasting statement of the meaning of democracy for the American people.

On January 1st, 1863, President Lincoln issued the Emancipation Proclamation, which freed the slaves. Two years later, the 13th Amendment of the Constitution ended slavery in all parts of the United States.

President Lincoln was assassinated on April 9th, 1865. He was shot to death while watching a play in Ford's theater in Washington, D.C. The assassin was John Wilkes Booth, an actor, who thought he was helping the South.

Exercises <small>(ANSWERS ON PAGE 165)</small>

I. Match words with similar meanings.

1. portrait	____	a. say no
2. admit	____	b. freedom
3. wrongdoing	____	c. tell the truth
4. elect	____	d. bring together
5. refuse	____	e. choose
6. conflict	____	f. with complete agreement
7. independence	____	g. fault
8. ideal	____	h. picture
9. unanimously	____	i. problem
10. unite	____	j. perfect

II. Cross out the word that does not belong.

1. a portrait >
   - a. painting
   - b. image
   - c. face
   - d. memorial

2. to admit >
   - a. a mistake
   - b. an error
   - c. a fault
   - d. a television

3. to refuse >
   - a. a wall
   - b. to eat
   - c. a gift
   - d. to sing

4. to elect >
   - a. a president
   - b. a spouse
   - c. a senator
   - d. a judge

5. to unite >
    a.   people
    b.   countries
    c.   a dress
    d.   states

6. a wrongdoing >
    a.   to help a sick person
    b.   to steal
    c.   to hurt someone
    d.   to lie

III. Select the word that best completes the sentence.

1. George Washington's (memorial, portrait, cherry tree) is in the White House.

2. President Lincoln was able to (ideal, unite) a country divided by slavery.

3. Lincoln's (ideals, independence) of democracy and freedom are admired by all people.

4. Washington couldn't lie; he (admitted, refused) chopping down his father's tree.

5. President Washington (refused, elected) to serve a third term as president.

6. The civil war was a tragic (conflict, ideal) during Lincoln's presidency.

7. According to a legend, Washington felt guilty about his (election, wrongdoing).

8. Washington fought to gain the (independence, conflict) of the United States from England.

9. Lincoln was (refused, elected) the 16th president of the United States.

10. Washington was the only president of the United States to be elected (independently, unanimously).

IV. Select words to complete the sentences below.

1. The artist painted both George and Martha Washington.

   Their _____ are on the wall in that museum.

2. The young couple finally came together.

   They were _____.

3. The friends talked about their problem instead of fighting.

   They resolved their _____.

4. The boys wanted the girl to represent the class.

   She was _____ to the job.

5. The young man told his friends he finally had met the girl of his dreams.

   She was his _____.

6. The young man decided to move out of his parents' house.

   He wanted his _____.

7. The mother told the children to eat the spinach, but they did not want it.

   They _____ to eat it.

8. The driver was afraid to say that the accident was his fault.

   He did not _____ he was wrong.

9. While playing in the street, the boys broke a window with their football and ran away. They were scared to

   admit their _____.

10. Everybody agreed Evelyn should be the treasurer. They elected

    her _____.

V. Ask a question about each statement. The first word in each question has been written for you.

1. John Singleton Copley painted a portrait of Paul Revere.

   What _____?

2. He admitted his wrongdoing because he couldn't lie.

   Why _____?

3. Lincoln was president during the the Civil War.

   When _____?

4. Washington became very famous during the fight for independence.

   When _____?

5. President Washington was elected unanimously.

   Who _____?

6. President Lincoln united the northern states and the confederacy.

   What _____?

7. In "The Gettysburg Address," President Lincoln expresses his ideals of democracy.

   Where _____?

8. George Washington was the first elected president of the United States.

   Who _____?

9. President Washington refused a third term.

   What _____?

10. George Washington's wrongdoing was to chop down his father's cherry tree.

    What _____?

VI. Use the Internet to get more information about Presidents' Day.

   1. Who was the president who decided to honor all the past presidents on Presidents' Day? Read and write an outline about it.

      http://www.infoplease.com/spot/washington1.html

   2. Find out about a president who interests you. At this website, click on his picture to find out more about him. Take notes. Write down his name, date of birth, place of birth, and the years when he was president of the United States.

      http://www.whitehouse.gov/history/presidents/

St. Patrick's Day

March 17, 20__

17

_____DAY

Traditions and Customs

On March 17th, many people in the United States commemorate St. Patrick, the patron saint of Ireland. New York City, where there are many people of Irish **descent**, holds the famous St. Patrick's Day parade. Bands, marchers, and **celebrities** (especially politicians) come to **participate**. More than 150,000 people march in the parade. Almost a million people line the streets to watch as **bystanders**. A green stripe is painted down the center of Fifth Avenue, and the lights on top of the Empire State Building are turned green, the color that represents the Irish people.

Millions of real shamrocks are flown from Ireland to the United States. They are used for decorations. Everything turns green on St. Patrick's Day. Green and gold **pennants** and green balloons are sold by the hundreds. Children and adults wear something green, and shops prepare green food: green bread, green pasta, green ice cream, green milkshakes. People eat corned beef and cabbage, and drink Irish coffee. Irish songs can be heard throughout the day on the radio.

St. Patrick in Ireland
www.catholic-forum.com/saints

Background

In Ireland, St. Patrick's Day is a religious holiday. St. Patrick's date of birth is **estimated** to be around the year 389. He died on March 17ᵗʰ, the day when his memory is honored.

When Patrick was 16 years old, Irish pirates landed near his home in England. They **captured** him and took him as a slave to Ireland. There he worked and learned the Irish language, traditions, and way of life. Patrick, who had been born and raised in a Christian home, was troubled because the Irish worshiped many gods and spirits. He wanted to **convert** the Irish people to Christianity.

He was able to escape to France and to study to be a priest. After 14 years of study, in the year 432, the Pope sent him back to Ireland as a bishop. Patrick traveled all across Ireland and established churches and schools. According to his followers he performed many **miracles**. A well known **legend** says that he drove the snakes out of Ireland. He was greatly loved by the Irish people.

This holiday in the United States has come to represent the Irish culture and the great contributions of its people to the United States. Last names beginning with "O'," like O'Reilly, and some names beginning with "Mc," like McSweeny, are of Irish origin. Many famous politicians, including Presidents Kennedy and Reagan, are of Irish descent.

Exercises (ANSWERS ON PAGE 165)

I. Match words with similar meanings.

1. celebrity	____	a. to take away by force
2. bystanders	____	b. story
3. participate	____	c. calculate, determine the size or number or value of something.
4. pennant	____	d. wonder; something out of the ordinary
5. estimate	____	e. take part
6. capture	____	f. famous person
7. convert	____	g. people who stand and look at something
8. miracle	____	h. flag
9. legend	____	i. origin
10. descent	____	j. to change a person from one religion or idea into another

II. Select the word that best completes the sentence.

1. Hundreds of (bystanders, celebrities) are standing along the avenue to watch the parade.

2. The students from the school band (convert, participate) in the St. Patrick's Day parade.

3. Saint Patrick wanted to (convert, estimate) the Irish people to Christianity.

A troupe of step dancers, adults and children, sponsored by the Cranbury Civic Arts Council, entertain at the St. Patrick's Day Spouse Night party given by the Cranbury (NJ) Lions

The Celtic Pipers won the 2004 First Place award for their performance in the Milwaukee, Wisconsin, St. Patrick's Day Parade

4. It is said that St. Patrick performed many (miracles, legends) in his lifetime.

5. Political (miracles, celebrities) join the celebration.

6. Green balloons and (pennants, estimate) are used for decorations on St. Patrick's Day.

7. It is (captured, estimated) that St. Patrick was born in the year 389.

8. St. Patrick was (captured, converted) by Irish pirates.

9. President Kennedy's family was of Irish (descent, legend); they came from Ireland.

10. Driving the snakes out of Ireland is a (legend, miracle).

III. Fill in the blanks.

Saint Patrick's Day is celebrated with a famous parade in New York City where there are many people of Irish _____. Many well known _____ participate in this event. The streets are full of _____ who come to _____ in the celebration. Everybody likes to wear green clothes that day. Green _____ hang from many windows. It is not known exactly when Patrick was born. It is _____ that he was born in 389. Patrick was taken away from his home as a young boy. He was _____ by Irish pirates. When he grew up he wanted the Irish people to abandon their worship of idols and to _____ to Christianity. After he studied religion he traveled across Ireland. People say that he did extraordinary things; he performed _____. There is a _____ that there are no snakes in Ireland today because St. Patrick drove them out.

IV. Use the best word to complete the sentences below. (Change to the past, as needed).

1. Rock _____ get paid a lot of money for their concerts.

2. A story that may or may not be true is a _____.

3. Many people were found alive after the earthquake; everybody said that it was a _____.

4. There is a mathematical formula to _____ pounds to kilograms.

5. The insurance investigator _____ how much money was lost in the fire; he said it was about $12,000.00.

6. When celebrities participate in a parade, thousands of _____ come to see them pass by.

7. A teacher wants all students to _____ in the lesson, so she calls everybody to the front of the room.

8. After a long investigation, the police _____ the criminal.

9. The school _____ was gold, blue, and red.

10. He says he is _____ from George Washington.

V. Cross out the word that doesn't belong.

1. bystanders people cars crowds

2. facts mysteries legends miracles

3. a sign a pennant a flag an idea

4. to convert to alter to change to observe

VI. Write an answer for each of these questions.

1. Who captured young Patrick?

   _____.

2. Was Patrick of Irish descent?

   _____.

3. Who participates in the St. Patrick's Day parade in New York?

   _____.

4. What do bystanders do?

   _____.

5. What color are the pennants that people buy and fly?

   _____.

6. What is another word for "guess?"

   _____.

7. According to his followers, what did St. Patrick perform?

   _____.

8. What is the legend about the snakes in Ireland?

   _____.

9. Who did St. Patrick convert to Christianity?

   _____.

VII. Use the Internet to find out about the history of the St. Patrick's Day holiday.

   www.historychannel.com/exhibits/stpatricksday/main.html

Easter

_____ __, 20__

SUNDAY

Traditions and Customs

For Christians, Easter is a religious holiday when they celebrate the resurrection of Christ. In the United States, Easter **coincides** with the beginning of spring. For many people, it is a time of **renewal**. It is a time to celebrate the end of winter and the beginning of the warmer season of spring.

Easter is always on a Sunday, but the date of Easter changes **yearly**. It is on the first Sunday after the first full moon on or after March 21, but it can never be later than April 25th.

During the Easter season, stores are decorated with traditional Easter **symbols**: Easter eggs, bunnies, yellow chicks, and flowers, especially Easter lilies. Many people also decorate the inside and outside of their homes. Easter **greeting cards** are a popular way to wish friends and relatives "Happy Easter." People also give Easter **baskets** filled with food and candy.

One of the traditional Easter activities is for children and adults to decorate eggs and give them as **gifts**. Chocolate eggs are also a popular gift for Easter. Other traditions related to Easter eggs are Easter egg rolls, a kind of race during which children try to roll uncooked eggs without breaking them, and Easter egg hunts. Real **dyed** eggs or plastic colored eggs are hidden in the home or in the lawn, and children have an exciting time hunting for the eggs. A popular egg hunt takes place in Central Park, New York City. There, children also participate in egg-and-spoon races and egg dyeing. Hundreds of people participate in this event. Children are told that the Easter Bunny hides the eggs for the hunt.

Every year there is an egg roll on the lawn of the White House, in Washington. Even the President and his wife join in the fun.

The Easter Bunny, a magical rabbit, is also a tradition of this season. Chocolate bunnies are very popular and can be found in many stores. To the delight of children and adults, people dress up as giant bunnies and appear at egg hunts and egg rolls.

Another popular celebration is the Easter **Parade**. A very famous parade takes place along Fifth Avenue in New York City. People walk along the avenue wearing colorful new spring clothes and fancy bonnets or hats. Anybody can participate in this parade. The avenue is closed to traffic, and many people parade with their pets or carry flowers, while others line the avenue to watch the parade.

Background

Most of the symbols associated with Easter represent **rebirth** and renewal. The egg has always been a symbol of the renewal of life. The rabbit has been revered by many cultures as a symbol of fertility and a bringer of new life. The first time the bunny appeared as a symbol for Easter goes back to the 1500's in Germany. The Germans also made the first edible Easter bunny in the 1800's.

The Easter basket is a tradition that comes from the old Catholic custom of bringing the Easter food to church to be blessed. Nowadays, the Easter basket is filled with sweets and toys.

It has become traditional to wear colorful clothes for the season. This is a way of saying goodbye to the cold weather, to the dark colors, and to celebrate the rebirth of the earth with its new flowers and fruits.

Exercises <small>(ANSWERS ON PAGE 165)</small>

I. Match each word with its meaning.

1. renewal	____	a. every year, once a year
2. coincide	____	b. a second birth, a new birth
3. yearly	____	c. a picture; an object that stands for something else
4. symbol	____	d. a line of marchers – bands, flags, floats
5. greeting card	____	e. beginning or starting again
6. basket	____	f. a printed card used to express wishes for special occasions
7. gift	____	g. a present; something that is given
8. dyed	____	h. colored
9. parade	____	i. to happen at the same time
10. rebirth	____	j. a container

II. Select the word that best completes the sentence.

1. I need to (rebirth, renew) my membership in the country club.

2. Bonnie said: "This year my birthday (coincides, greets) with Easter; they are both on the same day."

3. The Easter Parade is a (yearly, monthly) celebration.

4. Trees and plants have a (rebirth, rejoin) every spring.

5. It is a popular custom to send (greeting cards, symbols) for Easter.

6. Thousands of people watched the (holiday, parade).

7. Many painters prefer paints made with natural (dyes, dyed) for their artwork.

8. The white dove is a (coincidence, symbol) of peace in many cultures.

9. I sent my uncle a fruit (card, basket).

10. There's an old saying: don't look a (symbolic, gift) horse in the mouth.

III. Complete each of these sentences with one of the key words.

1. One of the traditional Easter activities is to hunt for eggs colored with different _____.

2. An old proverb is "Don't put all your eggs in one _____."

3. The new constructions in the neighborhood have _____ the area.

4. This city is experiencing a _____. It's going to grow, prosper, and come to life again.

5. The Easter season _____ with the beginning of spring. They both happen around the same time.

6. Birthdays happen every year; they are _____ celebrations.

7. Bonnets, colored eggs, and bunnies are _____ of Easter; when you see them you think of that holiday.

8. The _____ lasted for over two hours. It was very long.

9. The boy wanted to give his father a _____, so he bought him a book.

10. Some people buy lots of Christmas _____ because they want to send good wishes to friends and family.

IV. Discuss with the class and complete each line with appropriate examples.

1. Name four occasions during the year when you would send a greeting card:

   _____

   _____

   _____

   _____

2. What can you see in a parade?

   _____

   _____

   _____

   _____

3. Name two things that can experience a rebirth.

   _____

   _____

4. List four common gifts.

   _____

   _____

   _____

   _____

5. List four things that are put in a basket.

   _____

   _____

   _____

   _____

6. List three yearly events in your life.

   _____

   _____

   _____

7. List four things you can color with dyes.

   _____

   _____

   _____

   _____

8. Write two symbols of love.

   _____

   _____

9. In the United States, Easter coincides with the beginning of spring.

   a. Christmas coincides with the beginning of _____.

   b. The Fourth of July, Independence Day, coincides with the beginning of _____.

10. What do you need to renew this year?

   _____

   _____

V. Write questions that match the answers below. The first one is an example.

Example:
    Answer. Easter comes at the beginning of spring.
    Question: *When does Easter come?*

1. Answer: They are colored with dyes.
   How _____?
2. Children roll eggs on the lawn of the White House.
   Where _____?
3. People make Easter eggs and Easter baskets.
   What _____?
4. People wear colorful costumes because they like to celebrate the end of winter.
   Why _____?
5. The movie *Easter Parade* made the parade in New York City very famous.
   What _____?
6. People in colorful costumes and bonnets, people with pets and flowers, march in the parade.
   Who _____?
7. People send greeting cards.
   How _____?

VI. Use the Internet to find out more about Easter celebrations.

1. Find out about the history of the Easter Egg and the Easter Bunny.
   http://wilstar.com/holidays/easter.htm

2. Find out the dates of Easter for the next ten years. Prepare a chart with the information.
   http://wilstar.com/holidays/easter.htm

3. Find out how the date of Easter Sunday is determined.
   http://www.assa.org.au/edm.html#Method"

Mother's Day and Father's Day

May ___, 20___

_____
SUNDAY

June ___, 20___

_____
SUNDAY

Traditions and Customs

People in the United States honor their parents with two special days: Mother's Day, on the second Sunday in May, and Father's Day, on the third Sunday in June. These days are set aside to show love and **respect** for parents. Parents **raise** their children and try to educate them to be responsible citizens. They give them love and care. These two days also offer an **opportunity** to think about the changing **roles** of mothers and fathers. More mothers now work outside the home. More fathers help with child care.

These two special days are celebrated in different ways. People whose parents are dead visit the cemetery. On these days families **get together** at home, as well as in restaurants. They often have outdoor barbecues for Father's Day. These are days of fun, good feelings, and **memories**.

Another tradition is to give cards and gifts. Children make them in school. Many people make their own presents. Many people **value** them more than the ones bought in stores. They say it is not the value of the gift that is important, but it is "the **thought** that counts." Greeting card stores, florists, candy makers, bakeries, telephone companies, and other stores do a lot of business during these holidays.

A big kiss for Mom! There are an estimated 82.5 million mothers of all ages in the United States, according to the U.S. Census Bureau.

A father taking his young son fishing on Father's Day. According to the U.S. Census Bureau, there are two million single fathers.

Mother's Day was **proclaimed** a day for national observance by President Woodrow Wilson in 1915. Ann Jarvis from Grafton, West Virginia, had started the idea to have a day to honor mothers. She was the one who chose the second Sunday in May.

In 1909, Mrs. Dodd from Spokane, Washington, thought of the idea of a day to honor fathers. She wanted to honor her own father, William Smart. After her mother died, he had the responsibility of raising a family of five sons and a daughter. In 1910, the first Father's Day was observed in Spokane. Senator Margaret Chase Smith helped to **establish** Father's Day as a national commemorative day, in 1972.

Exercises (ANSWERS ON PAGE 165)

I. Match words with similar meanings

1. respect	____	a. gather; meet
2. raise	____	b. remembrances
3. proclaim	____	c. set; make permanent
4. role	____	d. bring up
5. opportunity	____	e. chance; time
6. get together	____	f. consideration, honor
7. memories	____	g. ideas
8. thoughts	____	h. cost; importance
9. value	____	i. declare
10. establish	____	j. a person's job, function, part

II. Select the word that best completes each sentence.

1. It is the responsibility of the parents to (establish, raise, smile at) their children.

2. Children must show (respect, memories, symbols) for their parents.

3. The traditional (raise, love, role) of mothers and fathers is changing.

4. Ann Jarvis wanted to (establish, work, respect) one day to honor mothers.

5. Most parents are not interested in the (respect, honor, value) of a gift from their children.

6. Mother's Day and Father's Day cards express loving (customs, thoughts, honors).

7. Most people who think about the past have happy (respect, memories, honor) of their parents.

8. Many families (remember, get together, establish) on Mother's Day.

9. President Wilson (honored, symbolized, proclaimed) a day to honor mothers.

10. These days are (symbols, roles, opportunities) to remember and honor parents.

III. Complete the sentences below.

Mothers and fathers are very important people in any society. They _____ their children from babies to young adults with love and care. They show their children the _____ they must play to be good citizens. They teach children to have consideration and _____ for others. Parents also make sure that children have good _____ to have a good education and develop their skills.

Parents work very hard to _____ a family. They try to set a good example, and in return they do not ask for much. They do not care about the _____ of gifts from their children, but they are happy with the _____ behind the gifts. Most people have happy _____ of their parents. It is a good idea that two days were _____ to honor fathers and mothers and give families a chance to _____ _____ and celebrate their lives.

IV. Complete the sentences.
  1. The actor played in different dramas.
       He played many _____.

  2. Nowadays students have lots of chances to develop their computer skills.
       They have lots of _____ to learn valuable skills.

  3. The couple was happy looking at the pictures from their wedding.
       It brought them happy _____.

  4. Their family meets every Sunday to have dinner.
       They enjoy _____ _____ once a week.

5. Alfredo took care of the kittens.

   He _____ them.

6. The two women agreed on their vacation plans.

   They had the same _____ about it.

7. The Congress of the United States declared a holiday to honor Martin Luther King, Jr.

   They _____ it a national holiday.

8. The bank opened a new office in Denver.

   They _____ another office.

9. The child showed admiration and consideration for her grandmother.

   She _____ her.

10. The famous painting was sold for a large sum of money.

    The painting was very _____ able.

V. Circle the word that does not belong.

1. to raise	to grow to	to bring up	to destroy
2. to establish	to set	to break up	to build
3. to value	to respect	to honor	to dislike
4. chance	no time	opportunity	favorable situation
5. to go away	to get together	to meet	to gather
6. books	remembrances	memories	thoughts
7. to tell	to declare	to be silent	to proclaim
8. thought	idea	action	concept
9. to value	to ignore	to appreciate	to like
10. group	function	role	job

VI. Make these statements negative.

Example: President Wilson established Father's Day.
President Wilson didn't establish Father's Day.

1. Maria's parents raised four children.

   _____.

2. Congress proclaimed it a legal holiday.

   _____.

3. She was wonderful in that role.

   _____.

4. Carlos had an opportunity to visit Rome.

   _____.

5. The Chan family will get together at New Year's.

   _____.

6. Trung has a strong memory of that event.

   _____.

7. My thoughts about that problem are positive.

   _____.

8. The value of this ring is more than a thousand dollars.

   _____.

9. He respected the law, and so he did the right thing.

   _____.

VII. Use the Internet to learn more about Mother's and Father's Day.

1. Find out about the history of Mother's Day.

   http://womenshistory.about.com/library/weekly/aa020506a.htm

2. Read and find out about the history of Father's Day.

   http://www.holidays.net/father/

Memorial Day

Traditions and Customs

Memorial Day is a **patriotic** holiday in the United States. It is also called Decoration Day. It is a legal holiday in most states. It is traditionally on May 30th but it is now observed officially on the last Monday in May.

Memorial Day is a sad holiday. The country remembers men and women in the Armed Forces who died or were **disabled** in war or in the **service** of their country.

People place flowers and flags on the **graves** of servicemen and servicewomen. There are ceremonies at Gettysburg National Military Park and at the Tomb of the Unknown Soldier in the National **Cemetery** in Arlington, Virginia. Tiny ships filled with flowers are placed on the Delaware River.

Wreaths are set afloat at Pearl Harbor, near the site of the battleship "Arizona."

Many organizations take part in parades and special programs. Some of these groups are **Veterans** organizations, Boy Scouts, Girl Scouts, and fraternal groups. The programs often include a reading of Abraham Lincoln's "Gettysburg Address."

Background

Memorial Day began during the American Civil War to honor the soldiers who died during the war. Some southern women chose May 30th to decorate the graves of the soldiers with flowers. It is also believed that Cassandra Oliver Moncure, a woman of French **origin** from Virginia, chose this date because it is the "Day of the Ashes" in France. (This French Memorial Day marks the return of General Napoleon Bonaparte's remains to France from St. Helena). In 1868, General John A. Logan designated the day to honor the soldiers who died in the Civil War by decorating their graves.

Since the end of World War I, Memorial Day has also been known as Poppy Day. The poppy has become the symbol of the **tragedy** of World War I and of the renewal of life because many of the battlefields of France bloomed with poppies. Little red paper poppies are sold to the public for the **benefit** of disabled and **needy** veterans. The money collected is used for medical and educational services. A tag on each poppy says: "Honor the dead by helping the living."

Exercises (ANSWERS ON PAGE 166)

I. Match each of these words with a definition.

1. patriotic	_____	a. very poor
2. disabled	_____	b. assistance
3. service	_____	c. loving one's country
4. grave	_____	d. unable to function normally; handicapped
5. cemetery	_____	e. the place where a person is buried
6. veteran	_____	f. very sad event, a disaster
7. origin	_____	g. a place with many graves
8. tragedy	_____	h. a person who has served in a war
9. benefit	_____	i. work done for others
10. needy	_____	j. background; place where a person or thing comes from

II. Match these words to words that best show the opposite meaning.

1. patriotic	_____	a. end
2. origin	_____	b. rich
3. needy	_____	c. receive
4. tragedy	_____	d. unpatriotic
5. beneficial	_____	e. not handicapped
6. disabled	_____	f. comedy
7. serve	_____	g. not helpful

2004 VFW Memorial Day Parade in Brewster, N.Y.

III. Choose the word that best completes the sentence.

1. People who cannot walk and need a wheelchair are (veterans, disabled).

2. Memorial Day honors men and women who died in the (origin, service) of their country.

3. She is a (patriot, veteran) of the Gulf War.

4. He is buried in Arlington National (Grave, Cemetery).

5. Cassandra Oliver Moncure came from a French family; she is of French (tragedy, origin).

6. Wars are a terrible (tragedy, benefit) because lives and property are lost.

7. During Memorial Day, money is collected for (patriotic, needy) veterans.

8. On Memorial Day radios play many (needy, patriotic) songs.

9. She decorated the (cemetery, grave) of her father.

10. Many people give money for the (benefit, tragedy) of disabled veterans.

IV. Complete each sentence.

1. The veteran had a very sad life; it was a _____.
2. The school has been fixed with special elevators and doors for the wheelchairs of _____ students.
3. My grandfather was a Civil War _____.
4. The Olympic Games are of Greek _____.
5. In the summer he worked in the _____ digging graves.
6. The family placed flowers on the _____ of their uncle, who was killed in the war.
7. Many organizations work hard to get money for _____ children around the world.
8. It's a _____ concert; the money will go for the children's hospital.
9. The National Anthem is a _____ song.
10. He _____ his country in war and peace.

V. Write questions about the sentences below. The first word has been written for you.

1. Memorial Day is a patriotic holiday.

a. What _____?

b. What kind of _____?

2. Memorial Day originated during the Civil War to honor the war dead.

   a. What _____?

   b. When _____?

   c. Why _____?

3. The old man placed flowers on his son's grave.

   a. What _____?

   b. Where _____?

   c. On whose _____?

4. They collected the money for the benefit of the needy.

   a. What _____?

   b. Why _____?

   c. For whom _____?

V. Use the Internet to find out more about Memorial Day.

1. Read to find out more about the history of Memorial Day.
   http://www.usmemorialday.org

2. Find out about the World War II memorial. What soldiers are remembered and honored there? Where is it located?
   http://www.wwiimemorial.com

Independence Day

July 4, 20__

4th

_____DAY

Traditions and Customs

On July 4th, the United States celebrates Independence Day. It is a legal holiday. It is called Independence Day because on July 4th, 1776, the Continental Congress **declared** that the United States of America would become **free** and independent from England. Many activities are **organized** to celebrate this holiday. All across America firecrackers are exploded and fireworks are displayed. They symbolize the gunpowder of the American Revolution. Bands play patriotic marches in parades. Politicians make speeches about freedom and American ideals.

There are patriotic readings and music at various parks. People organize street fairs. Planes from the Air Force **perform** acrobatics in the air. Picnics, clambakes, and barbecues are very popular activities on this day. Many families and friends celebrate the day at beaches, pools, and baseball games. The lights of the Empire State building in New York City display the colors of the American flag: red, white, and blue.

A woman dressed for the 4th. The Buckaroo's float in Bear Valley Springs. An old soldier remembers his comrades. Girls of the Stormy Knights Drum and Bugle Corps, South Hampton.

In Monticello, Thomas Jefferson's home in Charlottesville, Virginia, Independence Day is observed with a **naturalization** ceremony. Immigrants are **sworn in** and become U. S. citizens. In Boston, the birthplace of the American Revolution, the Fourth is celebrated with an outdoor musical performance. The Boston Pops Orchestra plays popular and patriotic music on the banks of the Charles River. The concert ends with cannons joining the orchestra in Tchaikovsky's *1812 Overture*, as fireworks explode over the river.

Background

In 1773, there were 13 English colonies in America, where more than two million people lived. England owned and governed the colonies. England tried to collect more money from the colonies by passing tax laws. These taxes made the Americans very angry. They said it was not fair for England to make them pay taxes that they did not vote on. The Americans said, "No taxation without **representation**."

One of the most hated taxes was a tax on tea. When three English ships loaded with tea docked in Boston Harbor, some Americans dressed as Indians threw all the tea into the water. This became known as the "Boston Tea Party."

England sent soldiers to America to **force** the colonists to **obey** English laws. English soldiers killed Americans in what is called the Boston Massacre.

It was finally decided at the Contintental Congress that Americans should declare their independence. The Congress chose Benjamin Franklin, John Adams, Robert Livingston, and Roger Sherman to work on this idea. Thomas Jefferson was chosen to write the Declaration of Independence. It was signed on July 4th, 1776. Copies of the Declaration of Independence were read throughout the colonies. In Philadelphia, the Liberty Bell was rung to call the people to hear the reading.

After seven years of war with England, the American colonies finally won and were **recognized** as a united independent nation.

Exercises <small>(ANSWERS ON PAGE 166)</small>

I. Match words and phrases with similar meanings.

1. to declare _____ a. standing in for someone else
2. free _____ b. to do what others want you to do
3. sworn _____ c. to arrange; to establish
4. representation _____ d. to tell openly; formally
5. to obey _____ e. without restrictions, not limited
6. to organize _____ f. promised; pledged
7. naturalization _____ g. to accept; acknowledge
8. to force _____ h. becoming a citizen
9. to perform _____ i. to make something happen using strength
10. to recognize _____ j. to make or do, especially a service or show

II. Circle the word that best completes each sentence.

1. The Continental Congress (declared, obeyed, represented) the independence of the American colonies on July 4th, 1776.

2. England wanted the American colonies to (represent, obey, integrate) its laws.

3. People (force, organize, swear) many activities to celebrate Independence Day.

4. The American colonies wanted to be (naturalized, represented, free) from England.

5. Many aliens become citizens and are (sworn in, organized, proclaimed) in Monticello on Independence Day.

6. The American colonies did not want taxes without (declaration, representation, organization).

7. Every year there is a (declaration, organization, naturalization) ceremony at Monticello.

8. With the Declaration of Independence, the United States wanted to be (recognized, obeyed, naturalized) as an independent nation.

9. At the ceremony, the airplanes (performed, serviced, displayed) for the crowd.

10. England sent troops to (organize, declare, force) the American colonies to obey its laws.

III. Complete the sentences below.
  1. The candidate told the reporters that she was going to run for president.

     She _____ her intentions.
  2. The family went to the ceremony where they became citizens of the United States.

     They went to the _____ ceremony.
  3. The band played several patriotic songs at the festival.

     They _____ at the festival.
  4. The child did not want to come home for lunch. Finally the mother made him come.

     She had to _____ him to come to lunch.
  5. When the tourist saw the building she said "It is the Empire State Building."

     She _____ it.
  6. The people of the island want to have their own government.

     They want to be _____.
  7. The governor could not go to the rededication ceremony so he sent his assistant in his place.

     The assistant _____ed the governor.
  8. The new citizens promised to respect the Constitution of the United States.

     They were _____ as citizens.
  9. "Antonio, you have to do what your mother says," said the father.

     The father wants Antonio to _____ her.
 10. Anna prepared a list of guests, invited the people, and bought the decorations for the party.

     She _____ it.

IV. Cross out the word that doesn't belong.

1. declare	tell	announce	question
2. delegate	nobody	senator	representative
3. alien	citizen	American	naturalized
4. identify	recognize	forget	know
5. power	weakness	force	strength
6. benefit	performance	concert	show
7. do as told	obey	follow	disobey
8. organize	put in order	destroy	arrange
9. liberty	independence	freedom	dependence
10. sworn	promised	disagreed	agreed

V. Complete each sentence below.

1. Every state has _____ in Congress.
2. To drive safely you must _____ traffic rules.
3. It is easy to find what you want here. It is well _____.
4. The famous actor wore dark glasses and a wig because he did not want to be _____.
5. The police took the criminal by _____.
6. The community orchestra has been practicing for two months. Tomorrow they will give a _____.
7. When you enter the country you have to _____ the value of the gifts you are bringing in.
8. Now that Norma is _____ at last, she can make her own decisions.
9. Mrs. Martinez is studying to become a citizen. She hopes to have her _____ papers soon.
10. The spy was _____ to secrecy.

VI. Write questions about these sentences. Ask about the word or phrase that is in italics.

Example: *Antonio* was sworn in as our new representative.
_____*Who was sworn in as our new representative?*_____

1. The colonies wanted to be *free*.

   _____?

2. There were *thirteen* colonies.

   _____?

3. Franklin represented *the new nation*.

   _____?

4. The colonies refused to *obey* England.

_____?

5. The naturalization ceremony will be *in June*.

_____?

6. The UN is going to *recognize the new nation*.

_____?

7. _Lee was forced to admit his mistake.

_____?

8. The Organization of American States has an *office* in D.C.

_____?

9. The performance was held *in the Springfield Music Hall*.

_____?

VII.   Use the Internet to find out more about Independence Day.

1. Find out about the history of the Independence Day traditions.
   www.fourth-of-july-celebrations.com/html/traditions.html

2. Find this web site:
   http://www.web-holidays.com/july4

Then   Click on "menus and recipes"and look at some of the food recipes for the celebration of the Fourth of July.

Click on "Articles" and find the article about fireworks. Find out how fireworks work and the safety measures regarding the use of fireworks. Make a list of the safety measures that are recommended.

Labor Day

September ___, 20___

———————

MONDAY

Traditions and Customs

Labor Day is a legal holiday. It is celebrated each year on the first Monday in September. It was planned as a day to honor workers in America and to give them a long weekend holiday from work.

Labor Day is traditionally celebrated with parades, speeches, and recognition of the labor **unions**. Labor Day sales are a popular event held on this holiday. Barbecues and picnics are popular on Labor Day. They mark the end of the summer season. Schools usually open after this holiday. The unions want the public to know that the workers of America do an excellent job. Newspaper, magazine, radio, and television advertisements bring the **message** to the people: "Look for the Union Label," which means the product was made by workers who belong to a union.

Background

Labor Day was started in 1882 by a union called the Knights of Labor. The first celebration was a long parade followed by a picnic in New York City. In 1894 Congress made it a legal holiday.

In America, workers were not always treated well. In the early days of the 1800's, hundreds of thousands of immigrants from Europe came to the United States. They worked for very little pay. The owners of businesses and factories were able to get a lot of work for little money. They expected their employees to work 10 to 16 hours a day. Women and children worked more cheaply than men, and owners **hired** them for this reason.

In the 1880's, a fight for the workers was led by men who were workers themselves. They organized the workers into labor unions. The American Federation of Labor (AFL) was organized in 1886. Later the Congress of Industrial Organizations (CIO) was founded. **Wages**, hours of labor, and working conditions have improved since that time. Labor unions have **persuaded** the government and the states to pass laws that limit how many hours a week men and women can be **required** to work. The government also passed laws to establish the **minimum** wage — the least a worker should be paid. They have determined that child labor, as well as discrimination based on sex, religion, color, and national origin is now illegal. **Strikes** occur when people feel that there is wrongdoing. Everybody hopes for a fair and quick end of a strike.

American employers and workers of today face the problems of automation and **competition** of goods made in foreign countries where wages and costs are lower. Labor unions are helping to find **solutions** to protect American workers.

Exercises (Answers on page 166)

I. Match words with similar meanings.

1. strike	_____	a.	pay
2. to hire	_____	b.	to need; to demand
3. wages	_____	c.	convince
4. persuade	_____	d.	smallest possible
5. to require	_____	e.	answer to a problem
6. minimum	_____	f.	to give a job
7. union	_____	g.	information
8. competition	_____	h.	stopping of work
9. solution	_____	i.	rivalry; contest
10. message	_____	j.	organization of workers

II. Select the word that best completes each sentence.

1. "Look for the Union Label" is a (solution, message) from the unions.

2.   Employers cannot (hire, improve) children to work.

3. Cars from Europe create (strikes, competition) for American workers.

4. Unions fought to have fair (wages, minimum) for all workers.

5. Labor unions work to find (messages, solutions) to the problems of American workers.

6. It is not legal to pay workers less than the (organized, minimum) wage.

7. The unions (persuaded, hired) the government to create laws to protect the workers.

8. Workers sometimes (strike, persuade) when they are unhappy about their salary.

9. (Improvements, Unions) are organizations made up of workers.

III. Complete these sentences.

1. The girl told her mother what her father had said.

   She gave the mother the _____.

2. The mechanic fixed the problem with the car.

   He found the _____.

3. The nurses are not working today because they are protesting against the long hours of work.

   They are on _____.

4. The company needed some new workers.

   They _____ two men and three women.

5. The worker went to the office on Friday to get paid.

   He went to get his _____.

6. The teenager explained to his father why he needed the car, and finally convinced his father.

   The teenager _____ his father.

7. Men have to wear a jacket and tie to go into that restaurant.

   Ties and jackets are _____ .

8. In some banks, people need at least $300 to open a savings account.

   The bank asks for a _____ amount of money.

9. The new worker became a member of the workers' organization.

   He joined the _____ .

10. Both stores sell the same merchandise and they fight for the same customers.

    They are in _____.

IV. Circle the word that does not belong.

1. to hire   to employ   to contract   to dismiss
2. to work   to strike   to protest   to demonstrate
3. salary   wages   work   fee
4. letter   message   communication   to know
5. to convince   to ignore   to prove   to persuade
6. competition   fight   agreement   conflict
7. solution   problem   agreement   answer
8. minimum   least   smallest   maximum
9. to demand   to need   to know   to require
10. union   organization   individual   group

V. Select the word that best completes each sentence.

hiring   persuading   requiring   striking   competing

1. Some high school students are trying to get a job at the supermarket.
   The supermarket is _____ new cashiers.

2. There are now smoking and non-smoking sections in restaurants.
   The law is now _____ places for smokers and
   non-smokers.

3. The teachers stopped working because they want more money.
   They are _____ outside the school.

4. "Look for the Union Label" is a message played on TV and radio.
   The union is _____ people to buy products made
   by union workers in America.

5. Korean companies are now exporting cars to America
   They are _____ with American companies.

VI. Write a sentence using these phrases.

1. on strike

   _____.

2. hired a

   _____.

3. the minimum wage

   _____.

4. persuaded him to

   _____.

5. required us to

   _____.

6. The Airline Employees Union

   _____.

7. They competed for

   _____.

8. the solution

   _____.

VI. Use the Internet to learn more about Labor Day.

1. Go to the Department of Labor (DOL) site. Find "About the DOL"; then find and click on the section on History and Resources. Finally click on the History of Labor Day. Read and make an outline of the history of this celebration.

   http://www.dol.gov/index.htm

2. Find the link to Labor Day Poetry and click on it. Then read the following two poems:

   a. "Always Finis." What is the poem telling the reader? Write a sentence about it.

   b. "I Hear America Singing" by Walt Whitman. Make a list of the workers Walt Whitman mentions in his poem.

   http://www.twilightbridge.com/hobbies/festivals/labor

Columbus Day

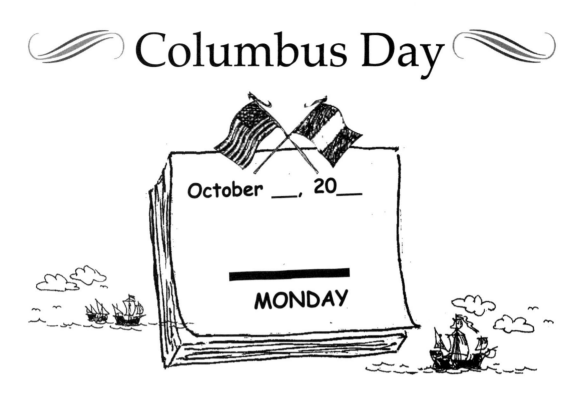

October ___, 20___

———
MONDAY

Traditions and Customs

Columbus Day is celebrated on the second Monday in October. It commemorates the discovery of America by Christopher Columbus on October 12, 1492.

In most places, banks, post offices, and other government offices are closed. Many schools hold programs and special events. Cities and organizations sponsor ceremonies, parades, fairs, food festivals, and banquets. Most stores are open and offer Columbus Day sales.

Traditionally this is a day to celebrate the **contributions** to the culture of the United States made by Italian immigrants. Pizza and pasta, opera, and Italian fashion are part of the daily life of Americans.

It is also a day to recognize the strong **ties** of friendship between the two countries: Italy and the United States. Italian-American politicians and entertainers participate in many public events and TV programs.

Background

Christopher Columbus was born in the seaport of Genoa, Italy. Columbus had heard about Marco Polo, who had visited the Far East 200 years earlier. Polo wrote about his long voyage by land and the wonders he had seen. Europeans became very interested in the gold, gems, and spices that came from the East. They used camels, horses, and elephants to travel on land, across mountains and deserts, to get to these countries. These trips were long, dangerous, and expensive. Columbus wanted to find a shorter **route** to Japan, China, India, and the East Indies.

At that time, many people thought that the world was flat. They said that if a ship would sail to the edge of the world, it would fall off and be lost. Columbus did not believe this; he was always **convinced** that the world was round.

King Ferdinand and Queen Isabella of Spain agreed to **finance** Columbus' **expeditions**. On the third of August, 1492, Columbus set sail with three ships, the *Nina*, the *Pinta*, and the *Santa Maria*. These ships were made of wood and had very few **comforts**. The ships had compasses, but they were small and **crude**. Columbus **navigated** by studying the stars and the moon.

Columbus, the great navigator and explorer, and a Taino man, one of the native people whom Columbus found on San Salvador. He called them "Indians." Soon he and his men began fighting the gentle Tainos and forcing them to work. In the next century most of them died, although Taino people survive today.

It was a dangerous voyage. Nobody had ever sailed so long without seeing land. Finally, on October 12th, they saw an island. Columbus believed he had discovered an island off the East Indies. He was wrong. He really had discovered a new world: America. He called this island San Salvador and the natives there Indians, because he was sure San Salvador was in the Indies.

As a seaman, he was one of the greatest in history. He not only discovered a new world, but his success **encouraged** other explorers. Later, because of Columbus, other sailors did find a new way to get to India.

Exercises <small>(ANSWERS ON PAGE 166)</small>

I. Match words or phrases with similar meanings.

1. contribution   _____   a. a way; a road

2. tie   _____   b. to provide money

3. crude   _____   c. to persuade someone to do or think something

4. to encourage   _____   d. something given to others

5. route   _____   e. to give help, courage, confidence

6. navigate   _____   f. something that holds people together

7. to finance   _____   g.   no pain; no worry

8. to convince   _____   h.   not refined; not carefully made;

9. expedition   _____   i.   to direct a ship or a plane.

10. comfort   _____   j. a trip of exploration.

II. Circle the word that best completes each sentence.

1. King Ferdinand and Queen Isabella (traveled, financed, convinced) Columbus' expedition.

2. Columbus was (comforted, navigated, convinced) that the world was round.

3. On Columbus Day we also celebrate the (contributions, expeditions, routes) of the Italian people and their culture.

4. There are (routes, comforts, ties) of friendship between Italy and the United States.

5. The instruments used in Columbus' expeditions were (comfortable, crude, financial).

6. The success of Columbus' travels (encouraged, comforted, routed) other explorers.

7. Columbus wanted to find a sea (navigation, tie, route) to the Indies.

8. The ships used for Columbus' expeditions had no (routes, comforts, finances).

9. Columbus (convinced, encouraged, navigated) his ships by studying the stars.

10. The King and Queen of Spain financed Columbus' (expedition, route, contribution).

III. Complete the paragraph.

Columbus was an explorer. He wanted to find a sea-route to the Indies. He needed money, so he talked to the King and Queen of Spain and _____ them to _____ his voyage. With the money, he got ships, equipment, and sailors for the _____.
The ships did not have many _____. The compasses were not sophisticated.

With the _____ compasses and the help of stars, Columbus _____ the ships. He did not get to the East Indies but he discovered a new world. His expeditions _____ other explorers to organize other expeditions.

IV. Cross out the word that doesn't belong.

1. Things to contribute to a party:
   a. money   c. food
   b. paper plates   d. sadness

2. Ties between friends:
   a. affection   c. secrets
   b. fights   d. understanding

3. Who can encourage?
   a. a parent   c. a teacher
   b. a friend   d. a competitor

4. You can organize an expedition to:
   a. your house   c. the moon
   b. a new island d. the Arctic

5. Somebody who can finance a new business:
   a. a banker   c. a businessman
   b. a rich person d. an explorer

6. You can convince:
   a. an argument   c. your husband or wife
   b. your friend   d. a teacher

7. Things related to comfort:
   a. noise   c. a soft bed
   b. beautiful music d. a quiet home

8. You can navigate:
   a. a ship   c. a bicycle
   b. a plane   d. a spacecraft

9. To be crude is to be:
   a. very simple   c. refined and sophisticated
   b. not well made d. unrefined

10. You need to know the route:
    a. to stay home c. to drive from Texas to Maine
    b. to go on a trip d. to sail from N.Y. to the Bahamas

V. Complete each sentence.

1. The music of Elvis Presley is part of American culture.

   Elvis made a _____ to American culture.

2. The father is giving confidence to his daughter by helping her learn to ride a bicycle.

   He is _____ her.

3. Albert is learning how to direct a plane.

   He is learning how to _____.

4. The young woman wants someone to give her money to start her business.

   She wants someone to _____ her business.

5. They are preparing the tools, maps, food, and instruments for the exploration trip.

   They are going on an _____.

6. Nancy didn't want to do it, but Rosa convinced her it was easy, and she finally did it.

   Rosa _____ Nancy to try.

7. The hotel was in a quiet place; the rooms were large, and they had a pool and a restaurant.

   The hotel had many _____.

8. The couple got a map and found the best way to go from Boise to Spokane.

   They found the best _____.

9. Ivan and Peter were friends for many years. They shared many things in their life.

   There were strong _____ between them.

10. The room was very simple. The table was just an old box.

    It was a very _____ table.

VI. Rewrite these sentences as negative sentences. Use contractions.

Example: This room is very comfortable.
This room isn't very comfortable.

1. Their company made a big contribution.

   _____.

2. Their art was simple and crude.

   _____.

3. He should have enouraged his brother to do that.

   _____.

4. They are taking a different route this time.

   _____.

5. He is going to be a navigator.

   _____.

6. The government could finance the expedition.

   _____.

7. Pablo convinced his father to go.

   _____.

8. Our hotel rooms were very comfortable.

   _____.

VII. Use the Internet to learn more about Columbus Day.

1. Go to: **www.infoplease.com/spot/columbusday1.html**
   Find the section about Columbus' Biography.
   Read to find out about his life.
   Make a timeline of major events in his life.

2. Go to: **www.mce.k12tn.net/explorers/explorers.htm**
   Find out about other famous explorers.
   Research an explorer who interests you.
   Write a paragraph about them.

Halloween

October 31, 20___

31

___DAY

Traditions and Customs

Halloween is a festival celebrated on October 31st. The name of the holiday means "hallowed" or "**holy** evening" because it happens the day before All Saints Day.

It is said that Halloween is the children's New Year's Eve. They dress up with special costumes, they eat too much, and stay up too late celebrating.

Children go around the neighborhood dressed in masks and colorful **costumes**. The most common costumes are witches, **ghosts**, skeletons, and popular TV, movie, and storybook **characters**. Some costumes are homemade; others are bought in stores. The children go door-to-door saying "**Trick** or **treat**." People give them candy, cookies, fruit, or money. Sometimes money is **collected** to help UNICEF (United Nations International Children's Emergency Fund).

Homes, stores, and classrooms are decorated in the traditional Halloween colors, orange and black. Usual decorations are jack-o-lanterns and colorful pictures of witches, black cats, ghosts, and skeletons. Jack-o-lanterns are pumpkins that are **carved** to look like faces. They are placed on doorway entrances and in windows. Horror movies and ghost stories are shown on TV on this day.

Adults and older children also celebrate Halloween with parades, festivals, and costume parties. Some people create their costumes; other people rent them. At some parties, there are contests, and the best costume receives a prize. One of the party events popular with children is bobbing for apples. Apples are put in tubs filled with water. People try to get the apples using only their mouths; hands cannot be used.

Background

Halloween comes the day before "All Saints Day." Many superstitions are connected with this day. The Druids, a group of priests from Gaul and Britain, believed that ghosts, spirits, and witches came out to harm people on Halloween. It is because of this legend that people place jack-o-lanterns and **scary** decorations in front of their homes to scare **evil** spirits away. The Druids also thought that cats were sacred. They believed that they were once humans who were changed into animals because they did evil things. That is why black cats are part of Halloween. It is also believed that the pumpkin symbolizes the human skull.

Exercises (ANSWERS ON PAGE 167)

I. Match words and phrases with similar meanings.

1. trick	_____	a. a person in a story, novel, play
2. to carve	_____	b. something harmful, bad
3. character	_____	c. a gift; something nice
4. collect	_____	d. a practical joke
5. evil	_____	e. frightening
6. holy	_____	f. to form something by cutting
7. ghost	_____	g. sacred
8. costumes	_____	h. to get; obtain
9. scary	_____	i. special dress
10. treat	_____	j. dead person's spirit

II. Circle the word that best completes the sentence.

1. Pumpkins are (carved, costumed, scary) to look like faces.

2. Some children dress like television (groups, characters, sets).

3. Children dress up to look like (tricks, saints, ghosts).

4. On Halloween you can see (collect, trick, scary) movies on TV.

5. Halloween means (evil, holy, scary) evening.

6. Children wear colorful (ghosts, characters, costumes) on Halloween.

7. Some children may play (tricks, treats, carve) on Halloween.

8. Some children (carve, trick, collect) money for UNICEF on Halloween.

9. People put scary decorations in front of their doors to scare (sacred, holy, evil) spirits away.

10. People give children (treats, tricks, costumes) when they come to the door.

III. Complete each sentence.

1. The girl bought a special dress for the.party.

   She bought a _____.

2. The child dressed up like a dead person.

   She wore a _____ costume.

3. When the birthday person opened the empty box, his friends laughed.

   It was a _____.

4. Martin liked to take a piece of wood and make a horse, cutting away with his knife.

   He liked to _____.

5. The book told a story about three people.

   The story had three_____.

6. One of the characters in the story was a bad, mean woman.

   She was _____.

7. The Bible is a religious book.

   It is a _____ book.

8. John has dozens of costumes.

   He has a fine _____ion of costumes.

9. The storm made everybody afraid.

   It was _____.

10. The father bought his son a large ice cream.

    That was a real _____ for the child.

IV. Complete the puzzle with words which mean the same as these words.

1. group
2. dress
3. person in a story
4. no danger

5. frightening
6. joke
7. bad

V. What are they doing? Complete each sentence with the words below.

carving   **trick or treating**   **scaring**   **collecting**

1. The teacher is cutting out a face on the pumpkin.
   She is _____ the pumpkin.

2. The children are putting the candy and money in a shopping bag.
   They are _____ the candy and money.

3. Children are going door-to-door on Halloween.
   They are _____.

4. Some people hang pictures of black cats and ghosts on their doors.
   They think they are _____ away evil spirits.

VI. Answer these questions with a sentence that uses one of the key words.

1. If you don't get a treat, what will you do?

_____.

2. What are you going to do to this pumpkin?

_____.

3. What are you going to wear for Halloween?

_____.

4. How do some children help UNICEF on Halloween?

_____.

5. What do children ask for when they go door-to-door?

_____.

6. What is she going to be, a ghost or a scary character?

_____.

7. How would you describe Frankenstein?

_____.

8. What does "sacred" mean?

_____.

9. What's another word for "very bad?"

_____.

VII. Use the Internet to learn more about Halloween.

1. Find out about the history of Halloween and who brought the jack-o-lantern to America.

http://wilstar.com/holidays/hallown.htm

2. Learn how to carve a pumpkin for Halloween. Make an outline of the steps and try to carve a pumpkin.

http://www.pumpkincarving101.com/

Election Day

Voting Requirements and Procedures

The first Tuesday after the first Monday in November is **Election** Day. In 1845 this date was set aside for elections by the US Congress.

On this day American citizens elect their public officials, president, congressional representatives, governors, mayors, and judges. A president is elected every four years, congressional representatives every two years, and senators every six years. In some elections, people can also **vote** on issues of public interest.

All states require that voters be citizens of the United States. They can be born in the country or naturalized. They have to be 18 years old by election day. Before they can vote, they must sign up with the local government. Voter **registration** rules may be different from state to state.

Polls are places where people go to vote. Polls are held in public buildings. The hours and places are **advertised** on TV and in the newspapers. At each polling place, election supervisors check the voter's identification. The voter then enters the voting booth. Inside the booth there is often a voting machine. There the voter votes alone and in secret, in the **privacy** of the voting booth. The names of the **candidates** and their political parties are listed on the machine. This list is called a "ballot." The voter chooses the candidate and then the machine counts the vote. Voting machines are helpful in getting fast **results** without mistakes. Candidates receiving the most votes are elected.

On the night of the election, people watch the election results on TV. When the results are final, they listen to the speeches made by the winners.

Background

The United States has two big political parties: the Democrats, symbolized by a donkey, and the Republicans, symbolized by an elephant. There are also several smaller parties. Each party has its own ideas about what is best for the country. The time before an election is when candidates **campaign**. They explain what they think, and what should be done. Candidates try to get the voters to vote for them.

This is also the time when it is the **duty** of the voters to find out as much as they can about the candidates and their plans. This can be done by listening to radio and TV news and **debates**, and by reading newspapers.

Exercises (Answers on page 167)

I. Match words or phrases of similar meanings.

1. election	_____	a.	an organized plan of action
2. to vote	_____	b.	what happened at the end
3. duty	_____	c.	the process of choosing leaders
4. registration	_____	d.	to express what you want
5. privacy	_____	e.	a formal discussion or argument
6. advertise	_f.	obligation
7. candidate	_____	g.	enrollment; being put on a list
8. result	_____	h.	not in public; secret
9. campaign	_____	i.	to tell people about something
10. debate	_____	j.	a person who wants to be elected

II. Circle the word that best completes the sentence.

1. The candidates for president usually discuss their ideas in a public (election, debate, result).

2. You have to wait for a(n) (election, voter, campaign) to vote for a candidate.

3. After the election, people watch the (voters, advertisements, results) on TV.

4. Candidates state their ideas during their (campaign, election, privacy).

5. People who want to be elected are called (voters, candidates, advertisers).

6. People who want to (advertise, campaign, vote) during the elections have to be citizens.

7. Before the election, it is the (duty, result, privacy) of the voters to find out about the candidates.

8. Newspapers, radio, and television (debate, vote, advertise) the date and time of the elections.

9. Before voters go to the polls they must go to a(n) (election, voting, registration) center.

10. Voting is done in (campaigns, debates, privacy); nobody can see what the voter does.

III. Complete each sentence with key words.

Election Day is in November. Newspapers, radio, and television

_____ the date and hours of the voting. On that day voters

go to _____ for their favorite candidates. Voting is done inside

a voting booth. Nobody can see who the person is voting for; voting is

done in _____.

Before _____ Day, candidates work hard in their

_____ trying to get the people to vote for them. Sometimes

_____ have a _____ on television before the

election. It is important to hear them and to find out as much as

possible about the candidates and their ideas; it is the _____

of the voters to know about the candidates. With the help of voting

machines and computers, the _____ of the election can be heard

and seen on the night of the election.

IV. Cross out the word or phrase that does not belong,

   1. choose   elect   vote   not decide
   2. poll   candidate   politician   campaigner
   3. privacy   secrecy   alone   public
   4. result   citizen   the end   consequence
   5. plan   strategy   campaign   election
   6. duty   job   obligation   treat
   7. debate   argument   discussion   advertisement
   8. advertise   publicize   keep secret   promote

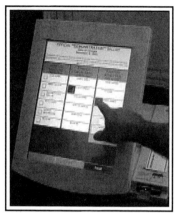

In 2004, Georgia citizens began using touch-screen voting machines. Here on its web site the Georgia Chronicle newspaper demonstrated choosing a candidate.

California voters also used touch-screen voting machines. Here a voter votes for a new law called a proposition.

V. Complete each sentence.

1. It is the _____ of parents to take care of their children.

2. You'll have to sign up for that at the _____ center.

3. The young girl wanted _____, so she closed the door to her room.

4. The children were playing outside all day, and as a _____ they were very tired.

5. The city organized a _____ to clean up the streets and parks.

6. The decision was unanimous; everybody _____ for him.

7. We don't have any candidates, so there won't be an _____.

8. The three candidates spoke in the _____ before the election.

9. There are two _____ for class president.

10. Makers of toys _____ in children's magazines and television programs.

VI. Use these phrases or words in a sentence.

Example: to elect > *We need to elect a new mayor.*

1. to vote>

_____.

2. to register >

_____.

3. to advertise >

_____.

4. to campaign >

_____.

5. to debate >

_____.

6. election >

_____.

7. results >

_____.

8. duty >

_____.

9. privacy >

_____.

10. candidate >

_____.

VII. Use the Internet to learn more about Election Day.

1. Read the answers to commonly asked questions about Election Day. Which answer was most informative for you?

http://www.fec.gov/pages/faqvdayeprocedures.htm

2. Find out how the Electoral College works.

http://www.calendar-updates.com/Holidays/US/election.htm

Veterans Day

November 11, 20___

11

_____DAY

Traditions and Customs

Veterans Day is celebrated on November 11th. It is a day to **remember** and **honor** all those Americans who served in the armed forces, and particularly those who fought during the Spanish-American War, World Wars I and II, the Korean War, the Vietnam War, and the Gulf Wars. People also remember the soldiers who are **missing** in action (MIA). This day reminds people of the **courage** and patriotism of all men and women who serve their country.

Veterans Day is **observed** with **ceremonies** at war **monuments** and cemeteries throughout the nation. Almost every village has a monument to veterans who served in one of the country's wars.

It is a day when many people visit national monuments such as the Vietnam Veterans Memorial, the World War II Memorial, the Korean War Memorial, and the Marine Corps Memorial in Washington, D.C.

Veterans groups organize barbecues, picnics, and dances. Store sales are very popular on this holiday.

Background

President Woodrow Wilson proclaimed November 11th as Armistice Day so Americans would not forget the tragedies of war. Great Britain and France also celebrate this day to commemorate the end of fighting of World War I on November 11th, 1918. On November 11th, 1921, the body of an American soldier killed in World War I was **buried** in the "Tomb of the Unknown Soldier" in Arlington National Cemetery in Arlington, Virginia. On the tomb are these words: "Here rests in honored glory an American soldier known but to God." Since then, unknown soldiers from more recent wars have also been buried at the tomb, now called the Tomb of the Unknowns.

A law **enacted** in 1938 made the day a federal holiday. In 1954 Congress changed the name to Veterans Day to honor all United States veterans. It is also a day **dedicated** to world peace.

Exercises (ANSWERS ON PAGE 167)

I. Match words or phrases of similar meanings.

1.	to remember	_____	a. no fear; valor; bravery
2.	to enact	_____	b. to celebrate
3.	courage	_____	c. to place a dead person in a grave
4.	missing	_____	d. to think of somebody or
5.	to observe a		something; to be reminded
	holiday	_____	e. to make official or legal
6.	to bury	_____	f. a formal occasion or service
7.	to be dedicated	_____	g. a memorial statue or structure
8.	to honor	_____	h. to have a single purpose
9.	monument	_____	i. to give respect
10.	ceremony	_____	j. lost, absent

II. Circle the word or phrase that does not belong

1.	remember	remind	forget	recall
2.	lost	absent	missing	found
3.	hide	bury	show	cover up
4.	establish	approve	deny	enact
5.	insult	honor	respect	love
6.	valor	bravery	fear	courage
7.	observe	forget	celebrate	commemorate
8.	ceremony	campaign	rite	event
9.	work for	be dedicated	care	trick
10.	ceremony	monument	structure	statue

III. Circle the word that best completes the sentence.

1. On Veterans Day, Americans (remember, bury, observe) veterans who served in the Armed forces.

2. There is a (monument, observation) honoring Civil War Veterans in the park.

3. People who fight for their country have (service, work, courage); they are not afraid.

4. After the war, many soldiers could not be found; they are (buried, dedicated, missing).

*HERE RESTS IN
HONORED GLORY
AN AMERICAN
SOLDIER
KNOWN BUT
TO GOD*

-Arlington Cemetery

5. Laying the wreath on the tomb was part of a very solemn (observation, honor, ceremony).

6. Veterans Day is (honored, named, observed) on November 11th in the United States.

7. The bodies of unknown American soldiers are (named, buried, dedicated) in the Tomb of the Unknowns in Arlington.

8. Many people all over the world are (named, celebrated, dedicated) to peace.

9. On Veterans Day, the United States (honors, buries, misses) Americans who served and fought for their country.

10. Veterans Day was established as a federal holiday by a law (enacted, named, observed) in 1938.

IV. Complete the sentences.

1. On Veterans Day, people also think about soldiers who did not come back or who could not be found.

    These are called soldiers _____ in action.

2. An American soldier's body was placed in the Tomb of the Unknowns.

    He was _____ in the tomb.

3. In 1938, Congress decided by law to observe Veterans Day on November 11th.

    They _____ the law.

4. Veterans Day is a day to think about people who served their country.

    It is a day to _____ them.

5. On this day, people remember that men and women serving their country are brave.

    They have _____.

6. Many people cried at the service.

    It was a sad and moving _____.

7. Veterans Day is celebrated with religious services, public ceremonies, and other events.

    It is _____ in many different ways.

8. Many organizations are working for peace in the world.

    They are _____ to world peace.

9. We had our picture taken at the base of the new statue.

    It is our newest national _____.

10. Most Americans give respect and thanks to those who serve the country.

    They _____ them.

V. Complete these sentences.

1. Sometimes it is hard to _____ family birthdays. Many people write them in a book so they won't forget.

2. Sonia could not find her keys; they were _____.

3. Dogs like to _____ bones in the ground.

4. Some famous singers and artists work very hard for needy people.

   They are _____ to helping others.

5. People who climb mountains have no fear; they have a lot of _____.

6. Before a law can be _____, Congress has to vote on it.

7. To _____ your parents, you must show respect and love.

8. Most people in the United States _____ the end of the old year and the start of the new with a party.

9. The _____ was very short – only fifteen minutes.

10. From the top of the Washington _____ you can see the whole city.

VI. Use these phrases in a sentence.

Example: are remembered > *Veterans are remembered on Veterans Day*.

1. was enacted >

_____.

2. is observed >

_____.

3. are buried >

_____.

4. are dedicated >

_____.

5. are honored >

_____.

6. a quiet ceremony >

_____.

7. missing in action >

_____.

8. They served >

_____.

9. a courageous person >

_____.

VII.   Use the Internet to find out more about Veterans Day.

1. Read about the history of Veterans Day.
   http://www.patriotism.org/veterans_day/

2. Find the section about Veterans Day ceremonies at Arlington
   Cemetery in Virginia.
   http://www1.va.gov/pubaff/celebAm/vetday.htm

Thanksgiving

Traditions and Customs

November ___, 20___

THURSDAY

Thanksgiving Day comes on the fourth Thursday in November. It is a holiday celebrated throughout the United States. People of all **faiths** celebrate this day. They give thanks for the many **blessings** in their lives.

This is a family holiday. Families come together from far and near. In some places special religious services are held in the morning. Then comes the traditional **feast**. Turkey is the main dish. It is served with sweet potatoes, squash, cranberry sauce, and pumpkin pie. Apple cider is the drink of the day.

Football is the most popular game on this day. For many schools, the Thanksgiving Day game is the most important one of the year. Usually there are several football games to watch on TV.

Macy's department store holds its **annual** Thanksgiving Day Parade in New York City. Celebrities, floats, bands, and huge **balloons** shaped like famous storybook and cartoon characters appear in the parade. Santa Claus arrives at the end. His coming marks the beginning of the Christmas shopping season.

Stores, classrooms, and homes are decorated with pictures of turkeys, Pilgrims, and Indians, and with **wreaths** of dried flowers and vegetables. Horns of plenty are also very popular. Charitable organizations serve dinners to needy people. They also send baskets of food to the **elderly** and sick.

Background

The first Thanksgiving Day was celebrated by the Pilgrims in 1621. They came from England for religious freedom. They sailed from Plymouth, England, on September 16,1620. Their ship was called the Mayflower. They landed at Plymouth Rock, in Massachusetts, on December 26, 1620.

The first winter was a terrible time. There was much sickness and **starvation**. Native American Indians taught the Pilgrims how to plant, fish, and hunt – how to **survive** in America. The crops did well, and in the fall of 1621 the Pilgrims had a great **harvest**. They were very thankful and decided to celebrate with a feast. The Pilgrims invited their Indian friends to share this Thanksgiving feast.

Thanksgiving was proclaimed a national day of observance by Congress in 1941.

Exercises (Answers on page 167)

I. Match words or phrases of similar meanings.

1. annual   _____ a. to stay alive
2. elderly   _____ b. a large meal, a banquet
3. feast   _____ c. religions
4. harvest   _____ d. a circular arrangement of
                         flowers or dried flowers
5. blessings   _____ e. hunger
6. faiths   _____ f. happening every year
7. starvation   _____ g. a bag filled with air or helium
8. balloons   _____ h. old people
9. survive   _____ i. the collection of crops (fruits,
                         vegetables)
10. wreath   _____ j. good things

II. Circle the word that does not belong.

1. flowers	arrangement	wreath	food
2. hunger	starvation	need	abundance
3. annual	yearly	weekly	every 12 months
4. young	mature	old	elderly
5. harvest	collection	planting	gathering crops
6. happiness	blessing	problem	goodness
7. religions	games	faiths	beliefs
8. alive	survive	die	exist
9. banquet	feast	starvation	meal
10. balloon	ball	toy	feast

III. Circle the word that best completes each sentence.

1. On Thanksgiving Day some organizations prepare food for the needy and the (shoppers, Pilgrims, elderly).

2. In the parade we saw a huge (toy, balloon, band) of Garfield the cat floating through the air.

3. People of all (elderly, faiths, observances) celebrate this holiday.

4. The Pilgrims organized a (feast, wreath, faith) to celebrate their survival.

5. Thanksgiving is a(n) (annual, observance, feast) holiday celebrated by people of all faiths.

6. After the Indians taught the Pilgrims how to plant, they had a good (survival, harvest, wreath).

7. A prayer of thanks before eating is also called a (duty, blessing).

8. During the Pilgrims' first year in America, many (starved, survived, hungry) to death.

9. Thanks to the Indians, the Pilgrims learned to (feast, observe, survive).

10. It is traditional to decorate stores and homes with images of turkeys and Pilgrims, and (wreaths, balloons, floats) of dried flowers and plants.

A traditional Thanksgiving dinner.

IV. Complete each sentence.

1. The winter in Minnesota can be too cold for old people.

   It can be too cold for the _____.

2. People can die if they do not eat food for a long time.

   They can die of _____.

3. At his birthday party the room was filled with floating messages.

   There were lots of _____ in the air.

4. The flower shop sent a big circle made out of flowers, leaves, and a ribbon.

   They sent a _____.

5. The people who got lost in the mountains stayed alive for ten days without food.

   They _____ for ten days.

In Upton, NY, Red Cross volunteers prepare Thanksgiving dinner for 650 senior citizens, half of whom are homebound and half of whom will gather together to celebrate.

6. Birthdays are celebrated every year.

   A birthday is an _____ celebration.

7. Many workers come to the farms to pick fruit.

   They come for the _____.

8. The religious leader said a prayer for a successful festival.

   He _____ the celebration.

9. The family had a big dinner at Thanksgiving.

   They had a _____.

10. You can find people from many different religions in the United States.

    The United States has people of many _____.

V. Ask questions about the sentences below.

1. People of all faiths celebrate Thanksgiving in November.

   a. Who _____?

   b. When _____?

   c. What _____?

2. The most famous Thanksgiving event in New York City is the Thanksgiving Day Parade. At the end of the parade Santa Claus arrives. People watching the parade feel excited and happy.

   a. What _____?

   b. When _____?

   c. Who _____?

   d. How _____?

   e. Which Thanksgiving event _____?

3. Charitable organizations send food to the needy and elderly.

   a. What kind _____?

b. What _____?

c. To whom _____?

4. Thanksgiving was proclaimed a national day of observance by Congress in 1941.

   a. What _____?

   b. When _____?

   c. By whom _____?

   d. Which holiday _____?

VI. Use the Internet to find out more about Thanksgiving.

   1. Read about planning for a Thanksgiving meal. Make your own plan and menu.
      http://busycooks.about.com/library/weekly/aa103000.htm

   2. Find out more about the history and traditions of Thanksgiving.
      http://www.thanksgiving-traditions.com

   3. Find out how early civilizations celebrated and gave thanks for the harvest.
      http://www.holidays.net/thanksgiving/story.htm

Christmas

December 25, 20__

25

_____DAY

Traditions and Customs

Christmas is basically a Christian religious holiday. It is also a day on which families come together to **share** their happiness, and **exchange** gifts. In the days before Christmas, parties are held in schools, offices, factories, clubs, and homes. Stores are crowded with shoppers.

Cities and towns in the United States and Canada **sparkle** with bright lights and decorations. Churches, homes, schools, shops, and streets are decorated with Christmas trees and lots of colored lights. Store windows **display** gifts and Christmas scenes. The traditional colors for this holiday are red and green, and the red poinsettia is the Christmas flower. On Christmas Eve, the President of the United States turns on the lights of the Christmas tree near the White House and sends his greetings to the nation.

Families prepare for this holiday for weeks. The Friday after Thanksgiving marks the beginning of the Christmas shopping season when people buy gifts for each other. Some people make their gifts. They wrap them with bright paper and ribbons. They choose a tree and then decorate it with **ornaments** and lights. Houses are decorated with wreaths of holly, evergreens, and mistletoe. Christmas cards are sent to friends and relatives.

Santa Claus, also called "Father Christmas," is the symbol of Christmas for children. Children believe he lives at the North Pole and brings gifts for them on Christmas Eve. He flies through the air in a sleigh pulled by reindeer, and leaves gifts under the Christmas tree. Children also hang up their stockings and Santa Claus fills them with little **presents**.

People wish each other a "Merry Christmas" during this holiday season. In many states, people look forward to snow and a "white Christmas." Christmas carols are sung and played on the radio and in public places during this season. There are many shows on television called "Christmas Specials." *Rudoph the Red-Nosed Reindeer, Frosty the Snowman,* and *Miracle on 34th Street* are family **favorites**. *A Christmas Carol* by Charles Dickens is read aloud and put on as a play in many communities every year. Churches, organizations, and newspapers ask for **donations** of money and food for the needy. **Volunteers** from the Salvation Army stand outside stores collecting money for the needy. Hot meals are prepared and served to the poor and homeless.

Most schools are closed for a long **vacation** during the Christmas season. They reopen after New Year's Day. Many families go on trips during those days. Some people go south to the beaches to enjoy the ocean and the warm weather. Other people like winter sports and go to the mountains for skiing and other winter activities. Whether people go away or stay home, they all enjoy one of the most popular celebrations of the year.

Exercises (ANSWERS ON PAGE 168)

I. Match words or phrases with similar meanings.

1. vacation _____ a. a show; a presentation
2. to share _____ b. to give and receive something
3. to sparkle _____ c. a gift, usually money, food, clothing
4. donation _____ d. something or somebody liked very much
5. to exchange _____ e. a break from school or work for travel and play
6. ornaments _____ f. to use or enjoy something with other people
7. present _____ g. to shine, to be brilliant
8. volunteer _____ h. a person who offers to help
9. display _____ i. decorations
10. favorite _____ j. a gift

II. Circle the word that best completes the sentence.

1. The movie *Miracle on 34th Street* is a family (favorite, celebration, donation) during this holiday.

2. During Christmas the stores and the streets (display, sparkle, crowd) with lights.

3. It is traditional to buy and (celebrate, volunteer, exchange) gifts with friends and family.

4. The week between Christmas and New Year's is a favorite time for taking a (vacation, holiday, event).

5. Christmas is a time to (receive, donate, share) the good things you have with others.

6. Many organizations collect (displays, donations, ornaments) for the needy.

7. In the morning, children find lots of (stockings, balloons, presents) under the Christmas tree.

8. People stop in front of the store windows to see the (displays, favorites, sparkle) specially prepared for Christmas.

9. Christmas trees are decorated with lights and other (sparkles, displays, ornaments).

10. Many (crowds, needy, volunteers) collect money for the poor.

III. Complete each sentence.

1. The boy gave a piece of his sandwich to his friend.

    He _____ the sandwich.

2. The stars were shining in the sky at night.

    The stars _____ .

3. The merchant gave $500 to the Salvation Army.

    He _____ed a large amount of money.

4. The ski area was crowded with people during the holidays.

    Many families were taking a _____ .

5. Manuel liked chocolate cake more than all other cakes.

    It was his _____ .

6. The family hung all the Christmas cards they received on the window so everybody could see them.

    The family _____ the cards.

7. The children bought little toys, bells, and lights to decorate the Christmas tree.

    The children bought _____ .

8. Many people help collect money for the needy. They help without being paid.

    They are _____ .

9. Her husband spent hours and a lot of money to buy something for his wife.

    He bought her a valuable and beautiful _____ .

10. During Christmas, people give gifts, and they also receive gifts.

    They _____ gifts.

IV. Complete the sentences.

1. In a small store, there is not enough space to _____ all the products so people can see them.

2. Next year we're going to go to Hawaii for our _____.

3. The skirt was too small, so the woman went to the store to _____ it for another one.

4. The children bought _____ for their parents.

5. Abdul gave Mary red roses for her birthday because they were her _____ flowers.

6. Everybody at the picnic put the food on a big table to _____ it with others.

7. The house was _____ because all the lights were on for the party.

8. The sign said " _____ for the needy will be gratefully accepted."

9. Ernesto went to buy _____ to decorate the Christmas tree.

10. There are many _____ helping to collect money for charity.

V. Ask questions about each sentence.

1. This summer the Sanchez family is going camping in the Rocky Mountains because it's less expensive than the Caribbean.

    a. Where _____ ?

    b. Why _____ ?

    c. When _____ ?

2. During the Christmas holiday, the streets are crowded with people shopping and looking at the stores' displays.

    a. When _____ ?

    b. Who _____ ?

    c. What _____ ?

3. People celebrate Christmas by getting together with relatives and friends to exchange cards and gifts.

    a. How _____ ?

    b. Why _____ ?

    c. With whom _____ ?

    d. What _____ ?

VI. Use the Internet to find out more about Christmas.

1. Find out how Christmas is celebrated in countries around the world. Compare the celebration in the United States to the celebrations in two other countries.

    http://www.christmas.com/worldview/

2. Find out about the history and meaning of many of the Christmas traditions. Read the questions, click on them, and learn about them.

    http://people.howstuffworks.com/christmas.htm

3. Read and listen to popular Christmas songs. Click on Songs of the Season. Copy the words and learn your favorite song.

    http://www.night.net/christmas/

Birthdays

_____ __, 20__

_____ DAY

Traditions and Customs

In the United States most people celebrate their birthdays on the day of the month when they were born. Birthdays are celebrated with family and friends. **Invitations** are sent for a party. A birthday cake with candles is served. The number of candles represents the age of the birthday person. The **candles** are lighted. The person makes a **wish** and then blows out the candles in one breath so the wish will come true. People sing "Happy Birthday" and wish the person health and long life.

It is **traditional** to bring or send birthday cards and gifts to the birthday person. Many people send flowers. Other gifts can be clothing, books, records, or perfumes. There is a birthstone and a flower for each month of the year. These can also be **appropriate** gifts.

Parties for children are usually held at home. At children's parties, children wear birthday hats and get **souvenirs** from the birthday child. Sometimes birthdays are also celebrated at school in the classroom with classmates. A parent may bring **refreshments** for the whole class; some teachers ask for juice and cup cakes, others for fruit or vegetables. Some parties are **catered** at restaurants. They **reserve** a special room for the birthday group and supply the refreshments and decorations. Balloons are especially popular at birthday parties.

Some birthdays are special. In some families, girls have a special celebration for the sixteenth birthday, called "sweet sixteen." The eighteenth birthday is important because it is the legal voting age.

Some people want to celebrate the birthday of a relative or friend with a "surprise party." They organize the party, but they keep it a secret and the birthday person does not find out about it. When the person comes to the party everyone shouts "SURPRISE!"

It is nice to remember the birthday of family and friends. One way to show this is by sending a birthday card, making a telephone call, or sending flowers. Some people make contributions to **charities** in the name of the birthday person.

Exercises <small>(ANSWERS ON PAGE 168)</small>

I. Match words and phrases with similar meanings.

1. candle   _____   a. proper, suitable, satisfactory

2. wish   _____   b. to provide food for a party

3. appropriate   _____   c. a small remembrance, a memento

4. to reserve   _____   d. a message or note asking somebody to attend a party or event.

5. to cater   _____   e. an object that is lighted to produce a flame for light or decoration

6. souvenir   _____   f. help given to the poor

7. invitation   _____   g. something that you want

8. charity   _____   h. snacks to eat at a party

9. refreshments _____   i. to set apart for special use

10. traditional   _____   j. practices and beliefs that are passed from one generation to another

II. Circle the word that best completes each sentence.

1. The (souvenirs, candles) on a cake represent the age of the person.
2. It is a(n) (celebration, tradition, invitation) to bring birthday cards and a gift to the birthday person.
3. People make a (party, birthday, wish) before they blow out their birthday candles.
4. Each child at her birthday party got a(n) (souvenir, wish, invitation).
5. Flowers are (catered, represented, appropriate) gifts for a birthday.
6. Many "sweet sixteen" parties are celebrated at (reserve, catering, charity) places.
7. Some restaurants (reserve, celebrate, appropriate) a special room for parties.
8. (Caterings, Refreshments, Wishes) are often served at parties.
9. People send (charities, invitations, cakes) when they have a special birthday party.
10. Sometimes people give money to a (celebrity, charity, caterer) in the name of the birthday person.

III. Complete the sentences below.

1. His T-shirt says "I ♥ Niagara Falls."
   It is a _____ of Niagara Falls.
2. The birthday girl sent me a note inviting me to her party.
   She sent me an _____.
3. Pedro was ten years old.
   There were ten _____ on the cake.
4. At the my party there were lots of balloons and things to eat and drink.
   The _____ were delicious.
5. We gave money to an organization to help the poor.
   We gave money to a _____.
6. Before blowing out the candles, the boy is thinking about something he wants very much to happen to him.
   He is making a _____.

7. The parents decided to have the "sweet sixteen" birthday in a place that prepares and serves food and organizes parties.
   The party was _____.

8. The CD we bought for Nina was a good gift, and she liked it.
   It was _____.

9. The custom of celebrating a birthday with a cake and candles has existed for many generations.
   It is _____.

10. The restaurant keeps a separate room just for private parties.
    They_____ the room.

11. Wendy says to Manny, "Have a wonderful trip!"
    She is _____ him a wonderful trip.

IV. Circle the word that does not belong.

1.	food	snack	refreshment	sleep
2.	good	inappropriate	appropriate	correct
3.	gift	candle	light	flame
4.	want	wish	forget	desire
5.	provide	serve	celebrate	cater
6.	reserve	keep	give away	save
7.	souvenir	memento	candle	remembrance
8.	letter	invitation	party	note
9.	unusual	traditional	old	customary
10.	assistance	abandon	help	charity

V. Complete the paragraph.

The bride and groom planned their wedding. They visited many
_____ halls. They were looking for a large place because they
wanted to have a big celebration and lots of delicious _____.
Finally they found a catering hall that was _____. They
_____ the hall for the date of their marriage. They prepared a
list of people to invite. Some represented the bride's family, and some were
from the groom's family. They wrote and sent the _____.
They decided that the bride would wear her grandmother's wedding gown
because it was a _____ in her family. They prepared
everything carefully, and their wedding was very beautiful. Everybody
_____ them happiness and health.

VI. Use each of these words in a question.

Example: candles> *How many candles did you put on the cake?*

1. wishes >

_____?

2. appropriate >

_____?

3. reserve >

_____?

4. catered >

_____?

5. souvenir >

_____?

6. invite >

_____?

7. charity >

_____?

8. refreshments >

_____?

9. traditional >

_____?

VII. Use the Internet to learn more about birthdays.

Read about the History of Birthdays, and learn about birthday traditions around the world.

http://www.birthdayexpress.com/bexpress/planning/birthdaycelebrations.asp

Cultural Holidays

The United States is a country of immigrants. People from many countries have immigrated to the United States throughout history. They came from all the corners of the world to live and make a home in the United States. Many groups remember and celebrate their countries and their cultures with special holidays. Some of the holidays, such Chinese New Year, Cinco de Mayo, and Kwanzaa, have become very popular. Many people participate in the celebrations.

Chinese New Year

The Chinese New Year is celebrated on the first day of the First Moon of the **Lunar** Calendar. The Chinese Lunar Calendar is based on the cycles of the moon. It is different from the Western Calendar, which is based on the earth's journey around the sun. Because of this difference, the Chinese New Year does not fall on the same day every year. The beginning of the lunar year can be anywhere from late January to the middle of February.

The Chinese Lunar Calendar names each year after a different animal, in cycles of twelve. The legend says that twelve animals came to say **farewell** to the Lord Buddha, and that as a **reward**, he named a year after each animal.

New Year's Eve and New Year's Day are family celebrations. These are times of family reunions and of thanksgiving. It is traditional to bring a bag of oranges and tangerines when

These happy dragons paraded up and down the streets of the popular Chinatown district in New York City in 2004

Gung Hay Fat Choy!
Happy Chinese New Year!
2005 celebration at the Cottage School in Sharon, Massachusetts

visiting family and friends. Large meals and banquets are prepared to symbolize abundance and wealth for the family.

The entire home is cleaned before New Year's Day, but on New Year's Day, the brooms are put away. People are not supposed to sweep on that day because they can sweep away the good luck.

Lighting firecrackers on New Year's Eve is a traditional way to send away the old year and greet the new year. It is an old Chinese tradition that firecrackers scare evil spirits away. At the stroke of midnight all the windows and doors should be open to let the old year out. In many cities with large Chinese populations there are New Year's parades, lion and dragon dances, and firecrackers in the Chinatown area.

Cinco de Mayo

Cinco de Mayo is a Mexican holiday. It honors an 1862 Mexican army which fought The Battle of Puebla **against** a French army almost **twice** its size and won. The Mexicans were **defending** their country against a French invasion.

Cinco de Mayo parade in San Jose, California, in 2001

This holiday has become popular in the United States, especially in cities where many Mexican people live. This is an opportunity for Mexican Americans (Chicanos) to celebrate their **heritage**. People generally dress in red, white, and green clothing. These are the colors of the Mexican flag. Many families begin the celebration by going to church. They prepare special meals.

Parades are very popular. Floats, horses, and cowboys, and women, men, and children in colorful traditional costumes march in the parade. Mariachi bands help to make the celebration even more festive. Mexican-American leaders give speeches about their **ancestors'** bravery in battle. Cinco de Mayo is a day on which Mexican Americans express their **pride** in their culture.

Kwanzaa

Kwanzaa is an African American cultural holiday celebrated for seven days from December 26th to January 1st. This holiday **focuses** on the traditional African values of family, community responsibility, and culture. The holiday was created in 1966 by Dr. Maulena Karenga , a professor at California State University, Long Beach. He felt that it was important that African Americans connect to their African ancestors.

Traditional Kwanzaa meal, 2005

The word Kwanzaa comes from the Swahili language; it means the first fruits of the harvest. African tribes and communities come together to celebrate and give thanks for the harvest. They sing, dance, drink, eat, and give thanks for the fruits and vegetables of the earth. Kwanzaa is based on seven principles: **Unity**, Self Determination, Collective Work and Responsibility, Cooperative Economics, Purpose, Creativity, and Faith. Each day of the celebration focuses on one of the principles.

Kwanzaa's colors are red, black, and green. People decorate their homes with paper streamers, balloons, and other decorations in those colors. A candle holder with seven candles is a traditional decoration. It is called a Kinara. A Kinara has three red candles on the right, three green candles on the left, and a black candle in the middle. The seven candles reflect the seven principles of Kwanzaa.

Technical Sergeant Jennifer Myers, 66th Air Base Wing, lights candles in the Kinara celebrating Kwanzaa (First Fruits) in 2003 at Hanscomb Air Force Base, Massachusetts

Celebrations are held in homes, churches, community centers, temples, and mosques. A Kwanzaa feast is usually served on December 31st. The table must have fresh fruit and vegetables on a straw mat. There must be an ear of corn for each child present. During the meal, a Unity Cup that stands for togetherness is passed around, and everyone takes a sip. Gifts are traditionally exchanged on January 1st, the last day of Kwanzaa.

Exercises (ANSWERS ON PAGE 168)

I.   Match words with words and phrases with similar meanings.

1. farewell   _____   a. ability to think and do in a new way
2. reward   _____   b. concentrate
3. twice   _____   c. goodbye
4. defend   _____   d. prize, financial award
5. heritage   _____   e. tradition
6. pride   _____   f. about the moon
7. focus   _____   g. self-respect/self worth
8. ancestors   _____   h. protect
9. creativity   _____   i. people who came before you
10. lunar   _____   j. two times

II. Circle the word that does not belong

1. farewell	goodbye	hello	so long
2. reward	honor	prize	problem
3. to defend	to care for	to safeguard	to attack
4. heritage	future	history	tradition
5. pride	self respect	hate	dignity
6. twice	double	two times	three times
7. focus	concentrate	distract	look carefully
8. ancestors	ancient people	grandparents	children
9. create	imagine	use skillfully	copy
10. lunar	of the moon	30-day cycle	solar

III. Complete each sentence with the word that fits best.

1. The (solar, lunar) calendar is based on the cycles of the moon.

2. Beethoven composed wonderful music. He was very (imagine, creative).

3. All the lessons this week were about the holidays of different cultures. The teacher (defended, focused) on cultural holidays.

Proud Mexicans parade on Cinco de Mayo

4. Mexican people who participate in the Cinco de Mayo celebration honor their traditions. They feel (twice, pride) in their culture.

5. During Kwanzaa, African Americans honor the traditions of the people who came before them — that is, their (ancestors, participants).

6. The great tenor Luciano Pavarotti wanted to say goodbye to his audience so he gave a (reward, farewell) concert.

7. The family was upset when their dog Floppy got lost. They wanted to give a prize to anybody who found their pet. They made a sign that said: "$50 (price, reward) if you find our dog Floppy."

8. In 1862, France invaded Mexico. The Mexican people (participated, defended) their country and won the Battle of Puebla.

9. During cultural holidays people honor their history and traditions; that is, they celebrate their (reward, heritage).

10. We rang the doorbell two times because the sign said, "Ring (double, twice)."

IV. Fill in the blanks with the appropriate vocabulary words.

creative   celebrities   focus   pride   ancestors
farewell   reward   defend   heritages   twice

The Principal Retires

1. The principal of the high school retired after 35 years of work. The school organized a _____ party so everybody could say goodbye to her.

2. She was an extremely _____ administrator — always coming up with a good solution to problems.

3. She gave a farewell speech. She said that she wanted the students and teachers to care for the school so they can feel _____ in the school.

4. The principal was so emotional that she cried not once, but _____.

5. She said she did not need gifts because her best _____ was to see how many students succeeded and graduated.

6. The _____ of her speech was that people must defend their heritage by honoring their traditions.

7. She said that traditions were started by our _____, all those people who came before us.

8. The principal said that it is important to continue our different _____ by observing our cultural holidays.

9. She ended by saying that all the students should _____ the search for truth and freedom of speech.

V. Ask questions that match the answers below. The first one is an example.

Answer: Green is the color that represents Irish people
Question: What is the color that represents Irish people?

1. The Chinese New Year is in January this year.

   When _____?

2. Italian Americans like to celebrate their heritage on Columbus Day.

   Who _____?

3.   Kwanzaa celebrates African American heritage.

   What _____?

4. People usually wear red, green, and white clothing because they are the colors of the Mexican flag.

   Why _____?

5. Cinco de Mayo is popular in California, Texas, and Arizona because many Mexicans and Chicanos live in those states.

   Why _____?

6. The Chinese Lunar Calendar is used to determine the date of the Chinese New Year.

   What _____?

7. Chinese people celebrate the new year by eating special meals and exchanging gifts.

   How _____?

8. The Kinara has seven candles.

   How many _____?

VI. Use the Internet to find out more information about Cultural Holidays.

2005 Chinese New Year parade in Chinatown, Chicago

1. Read about how astronomers developed the Chinese calendar.

   http://www.chinapage.com/newyear.html

2. Read to find out why the French wanted Mexico. Prepare an outline of the different reasons.

   http://www.mexonline.com/cinco.htm

3. Read about the seven principles of Kwanzaa. Write down the African word and its English translation.

   http://www.afrocentricnews.com/html/kwanzaa.htm

4. Find out how the Kinara is different from the Menorah.

   http://www.tike.com/celeb-kw.htm

Religious Holidays

Since the year 1620, when the Pilgrims came to America looking for religious freedom, people from different faiths have lived together in the United States. Although there are many religious groups in the United States, Christianity, Judaism, and Islam are the **major** religions. Some of their holidays are described below.

✝ CHRISTIAN HOLIDAYS ✝

Christmas

Christmas is the celebration of the birth of Jesus Christ. Christians believe that Jesus is the son of God. Christmas is celebrated on December 25th.

The Christmas pageant at Northampton Presbyterian Church in Hampton, Virginia, tells the story of Christ's birth. Children act the parts of the angels, shepherds, and the three kings or Magi.

The Christmas story is told in the Bible. Shepherds were watching their sheep when an angel appeared to them. He told them that a savior, Christ the Lord, had been born in

Bethlehem. The shepherds went there to see him. The baby Jesus was born in a stable. His mother was the Virgin Mary, and his father was Joseph. Three Wise Men, called the Magi, followed a star until it led them to Jesus. The Magi, sometimes called the Three Kings, gave Jesus gifts.

Nowadays, the stable where Jesus was born is often represented by a nativity scene. These nativities are often displayed in front of churches. The scene usually has the star of Bethlehem, the baby Jesus and his parents, the Magi, the shepherds, animals, and the angels.

Easter

The Bible says that Christ died on the cross on Friday, but on Easter Sunday, he arose from the dead and went to heaven. Easter is preceded by 46 days during which people are expected to give up something they like, for example, a special food. This period is called Lent. It begins on a Wednesday, called Ash Wednesday. The last week of Lent is called Holy Week, and it starts with Palm Sunday. On this day Christians commemorate the entrance of Jesus into Jerusalem when the people greeted him joyfully as a savior laying palm branches at his feet. Good Friday is the **anniversary** of the Crucifixion. On that day Jesus was crucified and died on the cross.

Muslim Holidays

Ramadan

Ramadan is the holiest period in the Islamic year. It is the ninth month of the Muslim or Islamic calendar. This calendar is a lunar calendar and is eleven to twelve days shorter than the solar year calendar used internationally. For that reason Ramadan falls at a different time each year.

Ramadan is a month of fasting, devotion to God, reflection, and self control. During the day, people **fast**; they do not eat, drink, or smoke. The fasting starts at **dawn** and ends at sunset. It is a common practice to have a meal before dawn. At the end of the day the fast is broken with **prayer** and a meal after sunset. The fast ends after the last day of Ramadan.

Id-al-Fitr

There are two major festivals in Islam: Id-al-Fitr and Id-al-Adha. Id-al-Fitr is the festival of breaking the fast at the end of Ramadan. It is celebrated on the first day of the month of Shawwal, the 10th month of the Muslim Calendar. The fast of Ramadan is broken with special prayers and festivities.

On the first day of the festival it is customary to take an early bath, wear new clothes, eat something sweet, and go to the Mosque for Id prayers. Men traditionally wear white clothes. Houses are decorated, large meals are prepared, families **gather** together, friends visit one another, and gifts are exchanged. It is also traditional for Muslims to visit the graves of their relatives and give to the poor.

Prayer is an important part of all Muslim holidays, but some Muslims also pray five times every day, bowing their heads to the ground towards the holy Ka'ba in Mecca.

Id-al-Adha

Id-al-Adha is the second great Muslim festival. It is the Festival of Sacrifice. It commemorates the biblical story of Abraham and his son. Abraham was ready to sacrifice his son to show his faith in God. At the last minute God sent a ram to sacrifice instead of his son.

Id-al-Adha **occurs** in the last month of the Islamic calendar, and it continues for three days. If they can afford to, families sacrifice an animal and share the meat with neighbors and the poor. This festival coincides with the pilgimage to Mecca, called the Hajj. Muslims from around the world travel to that holy city to pray.

✡ JEWISH HOLIDAYS ✡

Rosh Hashanah and Yom Kippur

Rosh Hashanah commemorates the anniversary of the creation of the world. It is commonly known as the Jewish New Year. It is celebrated on the first and second day of the seventh Hebrew month, Tishiri, in September or October of the solar calendar.

Jews observe the holidays with prayers and traditions both at home and in their synagogues. Here the congregation of Ohr HaTorah in Los Angeles celebrates Yom Kippur.

The ten days that start on Rosh Hashanah and end with Yom Kippur are called the Days of Awe, or Days of **Repentance**. According to the religious tradition, all things are judged on Rosh Hashanah. During the Days of Awe, God writes the names of people on "books." He also writes who will live and who will die. These books are written on Rosh Hashanah, but people have a chance for God's forgiveness during the Days of Awe. This is a time of the year to look back at the mistakes of the past year, and to plan to make changes for the next year. It is a time of repentance, reflection, and spirituality. No work is permitted on Rosh Hashanah.

A popular practice of the holiday is to cast off the sins on flowing water. On the afternoon of the first day of Rosh Hashanah, people walk to a river and empty their pockets into the water. Many people throw crumbs of bread. This is a symbol for "casting off," or **getting rid of,** their sins.

Yom Kippur is the Day of Atonement. Yom Kippur is the last chance to demonstrate repentance and to **atone** for one's sins. On the day before Yom Kippur it is customary to have two festive meals, one at midday and another in the afternoon so people can prepare for fasting the whole day on Yom Kippur. The entire day is devoted to prayer. No work can be performed on Yom Kippur.

Passover and Hanukkah

Two other important Jewish holidays are Passover and Hanukkah. Passover is the commemoration of the Exodus of Jews from Egypt, after being slaves for many generations. Passover begins on the 15th day of the Hebrew month of Nisan and it lasts for eight days. It can fall in March or April.

Hanukkah is celebrated on the 25th day of the Hebrew month of Kislev, and it falls during November or December. Hanukkah commemorates the victory of the Maccabees over the Hellenistic Syrians, and the rededication of the temple in Jerusalem. The Jewish people think of this festival as a celebration of religious freedom.

Exercises <small>(ANSWERS ON PAGE 168)</small>

I. Match the words with similar words and phrases.

1. gathering   _____   a. correct, make right
2. occur   _____   b. throw away- discard
3. fasting   _____   c. very important
4. anniversary   _____   d. group of people
5. prayer   _____   e. happen
6. major   _____   f. annual celebration of an event
7. repent   _____   g. sunrise
8. atone   _____   h. to be sorry
9. get rid of   _____   i. not eating
10. dawn   _____   j. request or thanks to God

II. Complete each sentence with the most appropriate word.

1. During Rosh Hashanah people look at their past mistakes and try to (atone, forget) for them.
2. Christmas celebrates the (prayer, anniversary) of the birth of Jesus.
3. Most religions have a time of (fasting, ancestors) and prayer.
4. Muslims spend many hours (gathering, praying) during Ramadan.
5. Lent is a time for Christians to pray, (gather, repent), and do penance.
6. Id-al-Fitr and Id-al-Adha are two (fasting, major) festivals of Islam.
7. Family (gatherings, anniversaries) are a traditional way to celebrate holidays.
8. Before Yom Kippur, Jews empty their pockets into a river to (celebrate, get rid of) their sins.
9. Muslims fast from (evening, dawn) to sunset during Ramadan.
10. Easter (focuses, occurs) in the spring.

III. Give the verb forms of the these words. Example:

observance   *to observe   observing   observed*

NOUN   **VERB FORMS**

1. gathering   _____
2. occurence   _____
3. fasting, a fast   _____
4. prayer   _____
5. repentance   _____

IV. Complete the sentences with an appropriate word or phrase. You may use a different form. Example: *participate, participant, participation.*

1. The doctor told Alice that she could not eat anything before the surgery. She had to _____.
2. The elderly couple celebrated fifty years of being married. Their children had a big _____ party for them.
3. There were many people at the birthday celebration. It was a large _____.
4. They thought the meeting was in the afternoon, but it actually _____ in   the morning.
5. There was a flood in the basement of the house. It was a _____ problem because everything got wet.
6. The mother asked God for help. She _____ that her son would get well soon.
7. The last chance to _____ for our sins is tomorrow.
8. The family left on the trip very early in the day; the sun was just coming up. They left at _____.
9. The vegetables were left outside the refrigerator, so Janet threw them in the garbage. She had to _____ them.
10. Omar knew he had made a big mistake. He decided to _____ and ask for forgiveness.

V. Ask questions that can be answered with the sentences below. Use the key words when possible.

1. The largest gathering of people occurred at the Washington Monument.
   Where _____?

2. I fasted the whole day on Tuesday.

   When _____?

3. The student is praying to get good grades on his exams.

   Why _____?

4. The sinner wanted to atone for his improper actions.

   Who _____?

5. The sun begins to shine softly at dawn.

   When _____?

6. Marriage is a major event in a person's life.

   What _____?

7. After graduation the college student got rid of all his old books.
   When _____?

8. Christians should repent their sins during Lent.

   What _____?

9. At Thanksgiving time the whole family gathered at grandmother's house.
   Where _____?

10. The Garcias celebrate their anniversary in October, but the Hayeks' is in November.
    Which couple _____?

VI. Use the internet to find out more about religious holidays.

1. Find out why people use an evergreen as a Christmas tree, and why it is decorated.

    http://people.howstuffworks.com/christmas.htm

2. Find out about Easter celebrations around the world.

    http://people.howstuffworks.com/easter.htm

3. Find out the dates of future Islamic holidays.

    http://www.infoplease.com/ipa/A0760942.html

4. Find out details about fasting during Ramadan.

    http://www.factmonster.com/spot/ramadan1.html

5. Find out the dates of future Jewish holidays. Make a chart.

    http://www.infoplease.com/ipa/A0875655.html

A roast turkey served with bread stuffing and gravy is
the most traditional holiday meal in the United States.
It is the typical main dish at Thanksgiving,
called the Thanksgiving Turkey.
It is also popular at Christmas and Easter and
any other time a family sits down together for a big
holiday meal.

Appendices

Readings for the Holidays
The Star-Spangled Banner 150
The Pledge of Allegiance 150
The Declaration of Independence 151
The Gettysburg Address 152
M. L. King, Jr.'s "I Have A Dream" 153
J. F. Kennedy's Inaugural Address 155
'Twas the Night Before Christmas 156

Songs for the Holidays
Auld Lang Syne 158
The Battle Hymn of the Republic 158
We Gather Together 158
He's Got the Whole World 159
We Shall Overcome 159
Silent Night 159
Jingle Bells 159

Some State Holidays 160

Gifts for Holidays and Other Occasions 162

Readings for the Holidays

For some holidays there are appropriate readings which help explain the meaning of the day. Poems, great speeches, and religious writings are often read or recited by heart in public. Here are a few important readings often heard on King's Birthday, Presidents' Day, Memorial Day, The 4th of July, Veterans Day, and Christmas.

The Star-Spangled Banner
(The National Anthem of the United States)

Oh, say can you see, by the dawn's early light,
  What so proudly we hail'd at the twilight's last gleaming?
Whose broad stripes and bright stars, thro' the perilous fight,
  O'er the ramparts we watch'd, were so gallantly streaming?
And the rockets' red glare, the bombs bursting in air,
  Gave proof thro' the night that our flag was still there.
Oh, say does that star-spangled banner yet wave
  O'er the land of the free and the home of the brave?

Oh, thus be it ever when free-men shall stand
  Between their lov'd home and the war's desolation;
Blest with vict'ry and peace, may the heav'n-rescued land
  Praise the Pow'r that hath made and preserv'd us a nation!
Then conquer we must, when our cause it is just,
  And this be our motto: "In God is our trust!"
And the star-spangled banner in triumph shall wave
  O'er the land of the free and the home of the brave!

Francis Scott Key, 1914

The Pledge of Allegiance

I pledge allegiance to the flag of the United States of America and to the republic for which it stands, one nation under God, indivisible, with liberty and justice for all.

The Declaration of Independence
July 4, 1776

The Unanimous Declaration of The Thirteen United States of America

When in the course of human events, it becomes necessary for one people to dissolve the political bands which have connected them with another, and to assume among the powers of the earth, the separate and equal station to which the Laws of Nature and of Nature's God entitle them, a decent respect to the opinions of mankind requires that they should declare the causes which impel them to the separation.

We hold these truths to be self-evident, that all men are created equal, that they are endowed by their Creator with certain unalienable rights, that among these are life, liberty and the pursuit of happiness. That to secure these rights, governments are instituted among men, deriving their just powers from the consent of the governed, that whenever any form of government becomes destructive of these ends, it is the right of the people to alter or to abolish it, and to institute new government, laying its foundation on such principles and organizing its powers in such form, as to them shall seem most likely to effect their safety and happiness. Prudence, indeed, will dictate that governments long established should not be changed for light and transient causes; and accordingly all experience hath shown, that mankind are more disposed to suffer, while evils are sufferable, than to right themselves by abolishing the forms to which they are accustomed.

But when a long train of abuses and usurpations, pursuing invariably the same object evinces a design to reduce them under absolute despotism, it is their right, it is their duty, to throw off such government, and to provide new guards for their future security. – Such has been the patient sufferance of these colonies; and such is now the necessity which constrains them to alter their former systems of government. The history of the present King of Great Britain is a history of repeated injuries and usurpations, all having in direct object the establishment of an absolute tyranny over these states. To prove this, let facts be submitted to a candid world. . . .

The Gettysburg Address
Abraham Lincoln, 1863

Four score and seven years ago our fathers brought forth on this continent a new nation, conceived in liberty and dedicated to the proposition that all men are created equal.

Now we are engaged in a great civil war, testing whether that nation or any nation so conceived and so dedicated can long endure. We are met on a great battlefield of that war. We have come to dedicate a portion of that field as a final resting-place for those who here gave their lives that that nation might live. It is altogether fitting and proper that we should do this.

But in a larger sense, we can not dedicate, we can not consecrate, we can not hallow this ground. The brave men, living and dead, who struggled here, have consecrated it far above our poor power to add or detract. The world will little note nor long remember what we say here, but it can never forget what they did here. It is for us the living rather to be dedicated here to the unfinished work which they who fought here have thus far so nobly advanced. It is rather for us to be here dedicated to the great task remaining before us – that from these honored dead we take increased devotion to that cause for which they gave the last full measure of devotion – that we here highly resolve that these dead shall not have died in vain, that this nation under God shall have a new birth of freedom, and that government of the people, by the people, for the people shall not perish from the earth.

Just before the end of the war, in his **second inaugural address** 3/4/1865, Lincoln said:

With malice toward none; with charity for all; with firmness in the right, as God gives us to see the right, let us strive on to finish the work we are in; to bind up the nation's wounds; to care for him who shall have borne the battle, and for his widow, and his orphan – to do all which may achieve and cherish a just and lasting peace, among ourselves, and with all nations.

"I Have A Dream"
Martin Luther King, Jr.'s Address at the Lincoln Memorial, 1963

Five score years ago, a great American, in whose symbolic shadow we stand, signed the Emancipation Proclamation. This momentous decree came as a great beacon light of hope to millions of Negro slaves who had been seared in the flames of withering injustice. It came as a joyous daybreak to end the long night of captivity. But one hundred years later, we must face the tragic fact that the Negro is still not free.

One hundred years later, the life of the Negro is still sadly crippled by the manacles of segregation and the chains of discrimination. One hundred years later, the Negro lives on a lonely island of poverty in the midst of a vast ocean of material prosperity. One hundred years later, the Negro is still languishing in the corners of American society and finds himself an exile in his own land. . . .

I say to you today, my friends, that in spite of the difficulties and frustrations of the moment, I still have a dream. It is a dream deeply rooted in the American dream.

I have a dream that one day this nation will rise up and live out the true meaning of its creed: "We hold these truths to be self-evident: that all men are created equal."

I have a dream that one day on the red hills of Georgia the sons of former slaves and the sons of former slaveowners will be able to sit down together at a table of brotherhood.

I have a dream that one day even the state of Mississippi, a desert state, sweltering with the heat of injustice and oppression, will be transformed into an oasis of freedom and justice.

I have a dream that my four children will one day live in a nation where they will not be judged by the color of their skin but by the content of their character.

I have a dream today. I have a dream that one day the state of Alabama, whose governor's lips are presently dripping with the words of interposition and nullification, will be transformed into a situation where little black boys and black girls will be able to join hands with little white boys and white girls and walk together as sisters and brothers.

I have a dream today. I have a dream that one day every valley shall be exalted, every hill and mountain shall be made low, the rough places will be made plain, and the crooked places will be made straight, and the glory of the Lord shall be revealed, and all flesh shall see it together.

This is our hope. This is the faith with which I return to the South. With this faith we will be able to hew out of the mountain of despair a stone of hope. With this faith we will be able to transform the jangling discords of our nation into a beautiful symphony of brotherhood. With this faith we will be able to work together, to pray together, to struggle together, to go to jail together, to stand up for freedom together, knowing that we will be free one day.

This will be the day when all of God's children will be able to sing with a new meaning,

> "My country, 'tis of thee,
>
> sweet land of liberty, of thee I sing.
>
> Land where my fathers died,
>
> land of the Pilgrims' pride,
>
> from every mountainside, let freedom ring."

And if America is to be a great nation, this must become true. So let freedom ring from the prodigious hilltops of New Hampshire. Let freedom ring from the mighty mountains of New York. Let freedom ring from the heightening Alleghenies of Pennsylvania! Let freedom ring from the snowcapped Rockies of Colorado! Let freedom ring from the curvaceous peaks of California! But not only that; let freedom ring from Stone Mountain of Georgia! Let freedom ring from Lookout Mountain of Tennessee! Let freedom ring from every hill and every molehill of Mississippi. From every mountainside, let freedom ring.

When we let freedom ring, when we let it ring from every village and every hamlet, from every state and every city, we will be able to speed up that day when all of God's children, black men and white men, Jews and Gentiles, Protestants and Catholics, will be able to join hands and sing in the words of the old Negro spiritual, "Free at last! free at last! thank God Almighty, we are free at last!"

Inaugural Address
John F. Kennedy, 1961

We dare not forget today that we are the heirs of that first revolution. Let the word go forth from this time and place, to friend and foe alike, that the torch has been passed to a new generation of Americans -- born in this century, tempered by war, disciplined by a hard and bitter peace, proud of our ancient heritage -- and unwilling to witness or permit the slow undoing of those human rights to which this nation has always been committed, and to which we are committed today at home and around the world.

Let every nation know, whether it wishes us well or ill, that we shall pay any price, bear any burden, meet any hardship, support any friend, oppose any foe to assure the survival and the success of liberty....

In your hands, my fellow citizens, more than mine, will rest the final success or failure of our course. Since this country was founded, each generation of Americans has been summoned to give testimony to its national loyalty. The graves of young Americans who answered the call to service surround the globe.

Now the trumpet summons us again – not as a call to bear arms, though arms we need – not as a call to battle, though embattled we are – but a call to bear the burden of a long twilight struggle, year in and year out, "rejoicing in hope, patient in tribulation"– a struggle against the common enemies of man: tyranny, poverty, disease, and war itself.

Can we forge against these enemies a grand and global alliance, North and South, East and West, that can assure a more fruitful life for all mankind? Will you join in that historic effort?

In the long history of the world, only a few generations have been granted the role of defending freedom in its hour of maximum danger. I do not shrink from this responsibility – I welcome it....

And so, my fellow Americans: ask not what your country can do for you – ask what you can do for your country.

My fellow citizens of the world: ask not what America will do for you, but what together we can do for the freedom of man.

'Twas the Night Before Christmas
or *A Visit from St. Nicholas*
Clement Clarke Moore

'Twas the night before Christmas, when all through the house
　　not a creature was stirring, not even a mouse.
The stockings were hung by the chimney with care,
　　in hopes that St. Nicholas soon would be there.

The children were nestled all snug in their beds,
　　while visions of sugar plums danced in their heads.
And Mama in her 'kerchief, and I in my cap,
　　had just settled our brains for a long winter's nap.

When out on the roof there arose such a clatter,
　　I sprang from my bed to see what was the matter.
Away to the window I flew like a flash,
　　tore open the shutter, and threw up the sash.

The moon on the breast of the new-fallen snow
　　gave the lustre of midday to objects below,
When, what to my wondering eyes should appear,
　　but a miniature sleigh and eight tiny reindeer.

With a little old driver, so lively and quick,
　　I knew in a moment it must be St. Nick.
More rapid than eagles, his courses they came,
　　and he whistled and shouted and called them by name:

"Now Dasher! Now Dancer!
　　Now, Prancer and Vixen!
On, Comet! On, Cupid!
　　On, Donner and Blitzen!

To the top of the porch!
　　To the top of the wall!
Now dash away! Dash away!
　　Dash away all!"

As dry leaves that before the wild hurricane fly,
    when they meet with an obstacle, mount to the sky
So up to the house-top the courses they flew,
    with the sleigh full of toys, and St. Nicholas too.

And then, in a twinkling, I heard on the roof
    the prancing and pawing of each little hoof.
As I drew in my head and was turning around,
    down the chimney St. Nicholas came with a bound.

He was dressed all in fur, from his head to his foot,
    and his clothes were all tarnished with ashes and soot.
A bundle of toys he had flung on his back,
    and he looked like a peddler just opening his pack.

His eyes – how they twinkled! His dimples, how merry!
    His cheeks were like roses, his nose like a cherry!
His droll little mouth was drawn up like a bow,
    and the beard on his chin was as white as the snow.

The stump of a pipe he held tight in his teeth,
    and the smoke it encircled his head like a wreath.
He had a broad face and a little round belly,
    that shook when he laughed, like a bowl full of jelly.

He was chubby and plump, a right jolly old elf,
    and I laughed when I saw him, in spite of myself.
A wink of his eye and a twist of his head
    soon gave me to know I had nothing to dread.

He spoke not a word, but went straight to his work,
    and filled all the stockings, then turned with a jerk.
And laying his finger aside of his nose,
    and giving a nod, up the chimney he rose.

He sprang to his sleigh, to his team gave a whistle,
    And away they all flew like the down of a thistle.
But I heard him exclaim, 'ere he drove out of sight,
    "Happy Christmas to all, and to all a good night!"

Songs for the Holidays

These songs are a small sample of the many folksongs, hymns, spirituals, and popular songs Americans enjoy on holidays. For certain holidays, many songs are sung; other days – Halloween and Columbus Day, for example – do not have well known traditional songs.

At Christmas, carols such as "Joy to the World" and "The First Nowell" are heard everywhere, as are popular songs such as "I'm Dreaming of a White Christmas," "Oh, Christmas Tree," "Rudolph the Red Nosed Reindeer," and "I'll Be Home for Christmas." On St. Patrick's Day, when all Americans become Irish, "My Wild Irish Rose," "When Irish Eyes Are Smiling," and"Sweet Rosie O'Grady" are sung among many old favorites. Patriotic songs like "Yankee Doodle," "It's a Grand Old Flag," "My Country 'Tis of Thee," and "America the Beautiful" are played by bands and sung by choruses on many occasions during the year. Although many Americans don't sing these songs themselves, they enjoy hearing them on the radio and TV.

Auld Lang Syne
(New Year's Eve)

Should auld acquaintance be forgot,
  And never brought to mind?
Should auld acquaintance be forgot,
  and days of auld lang syne?

For auld lang syne, my dear,
  For auld lang syne,
We'll take a cup of kindness yet,
  For auld lang syne!

by Robert Burns

The Battle Hymn of the Republic
(Patriotic Holidays)

Mine eyes have seen the glory
  of the coming of the Lord.
He is trampling out the vintage
  where the grapes of wrath are stored.
He has loosed the fateful lightning of
  His terrible swift sword.
  His truth is marching on.

Chorus: Glory! Glory! Hallelujah!
  Glory! Glory! Hallelujah!
  Glory! Glory! Hallelujah!
  His truth is marching on.

by Julia Ward Howe

We Gather Together
(Thanksgiving)

We gather together
  to ask the Lord's blessing;
He chastens and hastens
  his will to make known;
The wicked oppressing
  now cease from distressing,
Sing praises to his name:
  He forgets not his own.

Beside us to guide us,
  our God with us joining,
Ordaining, maintaining
  his kingdom divine;
So from the beginning
  the fight we were winning;
Thou, Lord, wast at our side,
  All glory be thine!

We all do extol thee,
  thou leader triumphant,
And pray that thou still
  our defender wilt be.
Let thy congregation
  escape tribulation;
Thy name be ever praised!
  O Lord, make us free!

He's Got the Whole World
(King's Birthday)

1. He's got the whole world
   in His hands (3 times)
   He's got the whole world in His hands.

2. He's got the wind and the rain
   in His hands (3 times)
   He's got the whole world in His hands.

3. He's got the little bitty baby
   in His hands (3 times)
   He's got the whole world in His hands.

4. He's got you and me, brother,
   in His hands (3 times)
   He's got the whole world in His hands.

5. He's got everybody here
   in His hands (3 times)
   He's got the whole world in His hands.

We Shall Overcome
(King's Birthday)

1. We shall overcome, We shall overcome,
   We shall overcome some day.

Chorus: Oh, deep in my heart I do believe
   We shall overcome some day.

2. We'll walk hand in hand,
   We'll walk hand in hand,
   We'll walk hand in hand some day.

3. We shall all be free, We shall all be free,
   We shall all be free some day.

4. We are not afraid, We are not afraid,
   We are not afraid some day.

5. We are not alone, We are not alone,
   We are not alone some day.

6. The whole wide world around,
   The whole wide world around,
   The whole wide world around some day.

7. We shall overcome, We shall overcome,
   We shall overcome some day.

Silent Night *(Christmas)*

Silent night, holy night,
   All is calm, all is bright
Round yon virgin mother and Child.
   Holy Infant, so tender and mild,
Sleep in heavenly peace,
   Sleep in heavenly peace.

Silent night, holy night,
   Shepherds quake at the sight;
Glories stream from heaven afar,
   Heavenly hosts sing Alleluia!
Christ the Savior is born,
   Christ the Savior is born!

Silent night, holy night,
   Son of God, love's pure light,
Radiance beams from Thy holy face
   With the dawn of redeeming grace,
Jesus, Lord, at Thy birth,
   Jesus, Lord, at Thy birth.

by Josef Mohr

Jingle Bells
(Christmas)

Dashing through the snow
   In a one-horse open sleigh,
O'er the fields we go
   Laughing all the way.
Bells on bob-tails ring
   Making spirits bright,
What fun it is to ride and sing
   A sleighing song tonight.

Chorus:
Oh! Jingle bells, jingle bells,
   Jingle all the way.
Oh, what fun it is to ride
   In a one-horse open sleigh!

Oh! Jingle bells, jingle bells,
   Jingle all the way.
Oh, what fun it is to ride
   In a one-horse open sleigh!

Some State Holidays

In the United States, a few of the states have official state holidays, and some other states observe unofficial state holidays. There are also a few special holidays that are not known nationally but are celebrated in specific states or by specific groups of people. Some of these special holidays, like Three Kings Day, are observed officially in one or more states but unofficially in others. Sometimes they have different names in different states – Three Kings Day is also called Twelfth Night, Old Christmas, or Epiphany. In the list below, when a state is listed, the holiday is an official state holiday in that state. The dates for holidays may always be the same (Three Kings Day is always January 6th) or may vary from year to year (Fast Day in New Hampshire is always the fourth Monday in April). The history of each of these holidays and its correct date in any specific year can be researched on the internet.

January 6	**Three Kings Day** – Puerto Rico
January 8	**Battle of New Orleans Day** – Louisiana
January 11	**De Hostos' Birthday** – Puerto Rico
January 19	**Confederate Heroes Day** – Texas
	Robert E. Lee's Birthday – Alabama, Arkansas, Florida, Kentucky, Lousiana, Mississippi, South Carolina
January	**Lee/Jackson/King Day** – Virginia (*third Monday*)
January 30	**Franklin Delano Roosevelt's Birthday** – Kentucky
February 12	**Lincoln's Birthday** – many states, also combined with Presidents' Day
February 15	**Susan B. Anthony's Birthday** – Florida, Minnesota
March	**Casimir Pulaski's Birthday** – Illinois (*first Monday*)
March	**Town Meeting Day** – Vermont (*first Tuesday*)
March 2	**Texas Independence Day** – Texas
	Ground Hog Day – unoffical nationally
March 17	**Evacuation Day** – Suffolk County, Massachusetts
March	**Youth Day** – Oklahoma (*first Day of Spring*)
March 22	**Abolition Day** – Puerto Rico
March 25	**Maryland Day** – Maryland
March 26	**Prince Jonah Kuhio Kalanianaole Day** – Hawaii
March	**Seward's Day** – Alaska (*last Monday*)
April 1	**April Fool's Day** – unofficial nationally
April 2	**Pascua Florida Day** – Florida
April 13	**Thomas Jefferson's Birthday** – Alabama, Oklahoma
April 16	**De Diego's Birthday** – Puerto Rico
April 15	**Income Tax Day** – official nationally – no holiday
April	**Patriots' Day** – Maine, Massachusetts (*third Monday*)
April 21	**San Jacinto Day** – Texas
April 22	**Arbor Day** – Nebraska - unofficial nationally
April 22	**Earth Day** (*internationally on the Spring Equinox*)
April 22	**Oklahoma Day** – Oklahoma
April 26	**Confederate Memorial Day** – Florida, Georgia; Alabama, Mississippi (*last Monday*)
April	**Fast Day** – New Hampshire (*fourth Monday*)

May 1	**May Day** – unofficial nationally
May 1	**Bird Day** – Oklahoma
May 8	(Harry S) **Truman Day** – Missouri
May 11	**Minnesota Day** – Minnesota
May 20	**Mecklenburg Independence Day** – North Carolina
June 3	**Jefferson Davis' Birthday** – Florida, South Carolina; Alabama, Mississippi *(first Monday)*
June 3	**Confederate Memorial Day** – Kentucky, Louisiana
June 14	**Flag Day** – Pennsylvania – observed nationally
June 9	**Senior Citizens Day** – Oklahoma
June 11	**King Kamehameha I Day** – Hawaii
June 15	**Separation Day** – Delaware
June 17	**Bunker Hill Day** – Suffolk County, Massachusetts
June 19	**Emancipation Day** – Texas
June 20	**West Virginia Day** – West Virginia
July 17	**Muñoz Rivera's Birthday** – Puerto Rico
July 24	**Pioneer Day** – Utah
July 25	**Constitution Day** – Puerto Rico
July 27	**Barbosa's Birthday** – Puerto Rico
August	**American Family Day** – Arizona *(first Sunday)*
August	**Colorado Day** – Colorado *(first Monday)*
August	**Victory Day** – Rhode Island *(second Monday)*
August 16	**Bennington Battle Day** – Vermont
August	**Admission Day** – Hawaii *(third Friday)*
August 27	**Lyndon Baines Johnson's Birthday** – Texas
August 30	**Huey P. Long's Birthday** – Louisiana
September 9	**Admission Day** – California
September 12	**Defenders' Day** – Maryland
September 16	**Cherokee Strip Day** – Oklahoma
September	**Indian Day** – Oklahoma *(first Saturday after the full moon)*
October 10	**Leif Eriksson Day** – Minnesota
	Oklahoma Historical Day – Oklahoma
October 18	**Alaska Day** – Alaska
October 31	**Nevada Day** – Nevada
November 4	**Will Rogers Day** – Oklahoma
November	**Oklahoma Heritage Week** - Oklahoma *(the week of the 16th)*
November 19	**Discovery Day** – Puerto Rico
December 7	**Delaware Day** – Delaware
December 13	**Santa Lucia Day** - unofficial nationally, Scandinavian
December	**Winter Solstice** - unofficial nationally, the shortest day of the year

Gifts
for Holidays and Other Occasions

People give gifts every year to their friends and family members at birthdays, wedding anniversaries, and some religious holidays. It is also a tradition to send a card to friends and business associates every year in December. In these cards they say "season's greetings," or they wish their friends a good religious holiday – "Merry Christmas" or "Happy Hanukkah" – and a "Happy New Year." On many other holidays, such as Mother's Day, Father's Day, Valentine's Day, Halloween, and Thanksgiving, people may give or send a card or small present to close friends or family members.

There are also special occasions when gifts are appropriate. Weddings, births, graduations, and housewarmings don't happen every year.

Weddings. Before a wedding, friends often have a party for the woman who is going to get married. It is called a wedding shower. It is typically only for women. The guests bring a gift for the woman's new home and sometimes a funny present, a joke. Also, just before the wedding, the friends of the groom are invited to a party for men called a bachelor's party. The guests are the men in the wedding party and a few other close friends. The groom often gives these guests a small present to remember the occasion. Sometimes brides have a similar bachelorette's party.

People often have formal weddings and send wedding invitations. Other couples prefer to be married quietly and informally in either a religious or legal, civil ceremony. After an informal wedding, the bride and groom often send a wedding announcement telling friends that they are married.

Friends who are invited to a formal wedding ceremony and the party afterward, called the wedding reception, send or bring a present. They send a present if they cannot come to the wedding. Friends who get a wedding announcement may also send a present. The wedding present is either something special that the bride and groom will keep to remember their wedding or a gift of money. To say thank you, the wedding couple will often give a small gift to their friends who are officially part of their wedding party. Sometimes they give an inexpensive token gift to everyone who comes to their wedding reception. The couple is expected to send a personal, handwritten thank-you note to everyone who has given them a wedding gift.

Births. Before a baby is born, friends of the mother often have a party called a baby shower. Like the wedding shower, this is typically only for women. The guests bring something for the new baby to wear or play with, or they bring something practical for taking care of the baby. Sometimes several friends will buy a larger present together, something expensive that the parents will need. A gift of money is also appropriate. New parents usually need it.

Illness and death. When people are ill, particularly if they are in the hospital, friends will often send flowers. When someone dies, friends often send flowers or make a contribution to charity in the dead person's name. It is important to send a thank-you note for these gifts.

Graduations. When people graduate from school, they often celebrate by sending announcements or inviting friends and family to a special party. It is very much like a personal holiday, particularly for high school and college graduation. Some families celebrate grade school, middle school, and graduate school graduation as well. The graduate is usually given something useful or some money.

Housewarmings. When people move to a new home, they sometimes give a party called a "housewarming" and invite their new neighbors, friends, and family. When they do, the guests at the party usually bring flowers, food, or something special and useful for the new house. Even when they do not give a party, the people in their new home will often receive gifts from friends and family, and new neighbors will bring a small gift of welcome.

Hostess gifts. When people visit a friend's home for a meal or to stay overnight, they often bring flowers or some special food or drink. This gift is sometimes called a hostess gift.

Holidays for gift giving. People give gifts for some holidays. They usually give gifts for the winter religious and cultural holidays – Christmas, Hanukkah, Il-al-Fitr, Kwanzaa, and Chinese New Year. For Valentine's Day, Easter, Mother's Day, Father's Day, and Halloween small gifts may be appropriate. If you are invited to a party at another holiday, it is polite to bring a hostess gift or to ask if you can bring something to eat or drink.

Typical gifts. Children are often given toys, books, videos, and clothes; adults typically are given books, music, clothes, and items for their home or office. Everyone appreciates gift certificates from a store. Flowers and special food are always appropriate for adult birthdays, anniversaries, and as hostess gifts.

Answers

Introductory Reading (PAGE 1)

I
1. legal
2. superstition
3. celebrate
4. religious
5. calendar
6. commemorates

II
1. superstitious
2. commemorative
3. illegal
4. celebration
5. legally
6. religion

New Year's Day (PAGE 7)

I
1. j
2. c
3. b
4. g
5. f
6. i
7. h
8. e
9. a
10. d

II
1. crowd
2. elaborate
3. floats
4. ancient
5. achieve
6. goals
7. embrace
8. resolutions
9. prosperity
10. toast

III
crowds
embrace
ancient
toast
goals
resolutions
prosperity
floats
elaborate

IV
1. toast
2. prosperity
3. ancient
4. goal
5. elaborate
6. crowd
7. achieve
8. embrace
9. resolutions
10. floats

Martin Luther King Jr.'s Birthday (PAGE 14)

I
1. e
2. j
3. g
4. i
5. h
6. c
7. d
8. b
9. a
10. f

II
1. memorial
2. segregation
3. integrated
4. discrimination
5. assassin
6. spiritual
7. clergyman
8. racial, rights
9. injustice

III
1. spirituals
2. injustice
3. clergyman
4. segregated
5. memorial
6. rights
7. racial
8. discriminate
9. assassin
10. integrated

IV
1. memorial
2. spiritual
3. racial
4. right
5. segregation

V
1. actor
2. democracy
3. separation
4. fireman
5. justice

Valentine's Day (PAGE 21)

I
1. b
2. c
3. g
4. d
5. i
6. e
7. f
8. j
9. h
10. a

II
1. a
2. d
3. a
4. c
5. c
6. c
7. b
8. c
9. d
10. d

III
1. decorations
2. romance
3. affection
4. spouses
5. companions
6. Merchants
7. feelings
8. humorous
9. festival
10. sweetheart

IV
1. romance
2. spouse
3. feelings
4. companion
5. festival
6. affection
7. humorous
8. sweetheart
9. merchants

V
1. romantic
romance
2. festive
festival
3. humorous
humor
4. decorated
decorations
5. affection
affectionate

164

Presidents' Day (PAGE 29)

I	II	III	IV
1. h	1. d	1. portrait	1. portraits
2. c	2. d	2. unite	2. united
3. g	3. a	3. ideals	3. conflict
4. e	4. b	4. admitted	4. elected
5. a	5. c	5. refused	5. ideal
6. i	6. a	6. conflict	6. independence
7. b		7. wrongdoing	7. refused
8. j		8. independence	8. admit
9. f		9. elected	9. wrongdoing
10. d		10. unanimously	10. unanimously

Saint Patrick's Day (PAGE 37)

I	II	III	IV	V
1. f	1. bystanders	descent	1. celebrities	1. cars
2. g	2. participate	celebrities	2. legend	2. facts
3. e	3. convert	bystanders	3. miracle	3. an idea
4. h	4. miracles	participate	4. convert	4. to observe
5. c	5. celebrities	pennants	5. estimated	
6. a	6. pennants	estimated	6. bystanders	
7. j	7. estimated	captured	7. participate	
8. d	8. captured	convert	8. captured	
9. b	9. descent	miracles	9. pennant	
10. I	10. legend	legend	10. descended	

Easter (PAGE 44)

I		II		III	
1. e	6. j	1. renew	6. parade	1. dyes	6. yearly
2. i	7. g	2. coincides	7. dyes	2. basket	7. symbols
3. a	8. h	3. yearly	8. symbol	3. renewed	8. parade
4. c	9. d	4. rebirth	9. basket	4. rebirth/renewal	9. gift
5. f	10. b	5. greeting cards	10. gift	5. coincides	10. greeting cards

Mother's and Father's Day (PAGE 51)

I	II	III	IV	V
1. f	1. raise	raise	1. roles	1. to destroy
2. d	2. respect	roles	2. opportunities	2. to break up
3. i	3. role	respect	3. memories	3. to dislike
4. j	4. establish	opportunities	4. getting together	4. no time
5. e	5. value	establish	5. raised	5. to go away
6. a	6. thoughts	value	6. thoughts	6. books
7. b	7. memories	thought	7. proclaimed	7. to be silent
8. g	8. get together	memories	8. established	8. action
9. h	9. proclaimed	proclaimed	9. respected	9. to ignore
10. c	10. opportunities	get together	10. valuable	10. group

Answers

Memorial Day (PAGE 57)

I	II	III	IV.
1. c	1. d	1. disabled	1. tragedy
2. d	2. a	2. service	2. disabled
3. i	3. b	3. veteran	3. veteran
4. e	4. f	4. Cemetery	4. origin
5. g	5. g	5. origin	5. cemetery
6. h	6. e	6. tragedy	6. grave
7. j	7. c	7. needy	7. needy / disabled
8. f		8. patriotic	8. benefit
9. b		9. grave	9. patriotic
10. a		10. benefit	10. served

Independence Day • The 4th of July (PAGE 63)

I	II	III	IV	V
1. d	1. declared	1. declared	1. question	1. representation
2. e	2. obey	2. naturalization	2. nobody	2. obey
3. f	3. organize	3. performed	3. alien	3. organized
4. a	4. free	4. force	4. forget	4. recognized
5. b	5. sworn in	5. recognized	5. weakness	5. force
6. c	6. representation	6. free	6. benefit	6. performance
7. h	7. naturalization	7. represented	7. disobey	7. declare
8. i	8. recognized	8. sworn in	8. destroy	8. free
9. j	9. performed	9. obey	9. dependence	9. naturalization
10. g	10. force	10. organized	10. disagreed	10. sworn

Labor Day (PAGE 71)

I	II	III	IV	V
1. h	1. message	1. message	1. to dismiss	1. hiring
2. f	2. hire	2. solution	2. to work	2. requiring
3. a	3. competition	3. strike	3. work	3. striking
4. c	4. wages	4. hired	4. to know	4. persuading
5. b	5. solutions	5. wages	5. to ignore	5. competing
6. d	6. minimum	6. persuaded	6. agreement	
7. j	7. persuaded	7. required	7. problem	
8. i	8. strike	8. minimum	8. maximum	
9. e	9. unions	9. union	9. to know	
10. g		10. competition	10. individual	

Columbus Day (PAGE 78)

I	II	III	IV	V
1. d	1. financed	persuaded	1. sadness	1. contribution
2. f	2. convinced	finance	2. fights	2. encouraging
3. h	3. contributions	expedition	3. a competitor	3. navigate
4. e	4. ties	comforts	4. your house	4. finance
5. a	5. crude	crude	5. an explorer	5. expedition
6. i	6. encouraged	navigated	6. an argument	6. persuaded /
7. b	7. route	encouraged	7. noise	encouraged
8. c	8. comforts		8. a bicycle	7. comforts
9. j	9. navigated		9. refined and	8. route
10. g	10. expedition		sophisticated	9. ties
			10. to stay home	10. crude

Halloween (PAGE 86)

I	II	III	IV	V
1. d	1. carved	1. costume	1. organization	1. carving
2. f	2. characters	2. ghost	2. costume	2. collecting
3. a	3. ghosts	3. trick	3. character	3. trick or treating
4. h	4. scary	4. carve	4. safety	4. scaring
5. b	5. holy	5. characters	5. scary	
6. g	6. costumes	6. evil	6. trick	
7. j	7. tricks	7. holy	7. evil	
8. i	8. collect	8. collection		
9. e	9. evil	9. scary		
10. c	10. treats	10. treat		

Election Day (PAGE 92)

I	II	III	IV	V
1. c	1. debate	advertise	1. not decide	1. duty
2. d	2. election	vote	2. poll	2. registration
3. f	3. results	privacy	3. public	3. privacy
4. g	4. campaign	Election	4. citizen	4. result
5. h	5. candidates	campaigns	5. election	5. campaign
6. i	6. vote	candidates	6. treat	6. voted
7. j	7. duty	debate	7. advertisement	7. election
8. b	8. advertise	duty	8. keep secret	8. debate
9. a	9. registration	results		9. candidates
10. e	10. privacy			10. advertise

Veterans Day (PAGE 99)

I	II	III	IV	V
1. d	1. forget	1. remember	1. missing	1. remember
2. e	2. found	2. monument	2. buried	2. lost
3. a	3. show	3. courage	3. enacted	3. bury
4. j	4. deny	4. missing	4. remember	4. dedicated
5. b	5. insult	5. ceremony	5. courage	5. courage
6. c	6. fear	6. observed	6. ceremony	6. enacted
7. h	7. forget	7. buried	7. observed	7. honor
8. i	8. campaign	8. dedicated	8. dedicated	8. observe
9. g	9. trick	9. honors	9. monument	9. ceremony
10. f	10. ceremony	10. enacted	10. honor	10. monument

Thanksgiving (PAGE 106)

I	II	III	IV
1. f	1. food	1. elderly	1. elderly
2. h	2. abundance	2. balloon	2. starvation
3. b	3. weekly	3. faiths	3. balloons
4. i	4. young	4. feast	4. wreath
5. j	5. planting	5. annual	5. survived
6. c	6. problem	6. harvest	6. annual
7. e	7. games	7. blessing	7. harvest
8. g	8. die	8. starved	8. blessed
9. a	9. starvation	9. survive	9. feast
10. d	10. feast	10. wreaths	10. faiths

Christmas (PAGE 114)

I	II	III	IV
1. e	1. favorite	1. shared	1. display
2. f	2. sparkle	2. sparkled	2. vacation
3. g	3. exchange	3. donated	3. exchange
4. c	4. vacation	4. vacation	4. presents
5. b	5. share	5. favorite	5. favorite
6. i	6. donations	6. displayed	6. share
7. j	7. presents	7. ornaments	7. sparkling
8. h	8. displays	8. volunteers	8. Donations
9. a	9. ornaments	9. gift	9. ornaments
10. d	10. volunteers	10. exchange	10. volunteers

Birthdays (PAGE 121)

I	II	III	IV	V
1. e	1. candles	1. souvenir	1. sleep	catering
2. g	2. a tradition	2. invitation	2. inappropriate	celebration
3. a	3. wishes	3. candles	3. gift	refreshments
4. i	4. souvenir	4. refreshments	4. forget	appropriate
5. b	5. appropriate	5. charity	5. celebrate	reserved
6. c	6. catering	6. wishes	6. give away	invitations
7. d	7. reserve	7. catered	7. candle	tradition
8. f	8. refreshments	8. appropriate	8. party	wished
9. h	9. invitations	9. traditional	9. unusual	
10. j	10. charity	10. reserve	10. abandon	
		11. wishing		

Cultural Holidays (PAGE 128)

I	II	III	IV
1. c	1. hello	1. lunar	1. farewell
2. d	2. problem	2. creative	2. creative
3. j	3. to attack	3. focused	3. pride
4. h	4. future	4. pride	4. twice
5. e	5. hate	5. ancestors	5. reward
6. g	6. three times	6. farewell	6. focus
7. b	7. distract	7. reward	7. ancestors
8. i	8. children	8. defended	8. heritages
9. a	9. repeat blindly	9. heritage	9. defend
10. f	10. solar	10. twice	

Religious Holidays (PAGE 138)

I	II	III	IV
1. d	1. atone	1. gathering, to gather, gathering, gathered	1. fast
2. e	2. anniversary	2. occurrence, to occur, ocurring, occurred	2. anniversary
3. i	3. fasting	3. fasting/a fast, to fast, fasting, fasted	3. gathering
4. f	4. praying	4. prayer, to pray, praying, prayed	4. occurred
5. j	5. repent	5. repentance, to repent, repenting, repented	5. major
6. c	6. major		6. prayed
7. h	7. gatherings		7. atone
8. a	8. get rid of		8. dawn
9. b	9. dawn		9. get rid of
10. g	10. occurs		10. repent

Suggestions for the Teacher

These readings and exercises can be used in a variety of ways, adapted and modified to fit your teaching situation. Some suggestions are outlined below. In general, the readings and their accompanying exercises may be used either for self-study out of class or for group study in class.

For Self-Study.

If the students are to use this book for out of class self-study only, orient the students to the book and how they are to use it. This can be done in the following way.

1. Go through the Introductory Lesson with the students (See the group study technique for one procedure). You should point out the redundant style of the readings and encourage them to get into the habit of trying to get at the meaning of a word from the context.

2. Go through the exercises with the students. Point out that there is an answer key, but that the next to last exercise does not have answers in the key. You can ask the students to submit their written answers to the last exercise to you on a regular basis, or have them show their answers to a native-speaker friend.

3. Encourage the students to check out one of the web sites.

For Group Study.

The basic technique and the variations described below can be used for any of the passages. You can also, to vary the procedure, do some of the passages as group study and some as self-study.

1. Refer to the table of contents and have the students look at the key words for the passage. Ask them to note which ones they think they know and which ones they're not sure of.

2. Go over the list of key words for pronunciation. You can pronounce the words and simply have the students repeat them or have the students read them aloud.

3. *Option A.* Have the students read the entire passage silently. Encourage them to try to grasp the meaning from the context.

    Option B. Have the students take turns reading the passage aloud. Note any pronunciation problems and correct them after everybody has read.

    Option C. You read the passage aloud while the students listen. This option can be done twice. First the students listen with their books closed; then when you read it the second time they can follow along in their books.

4. Have the students do the exercises individually. When they have finished you can ask for questions and clarify problems.

5. The next to last exercise asks students to use their own words and there are no answers at the back of the book. You can use this exercise as a test by having the students write out their sentences on a separate sheet of paper and hand them in to you.

6. If your students have access to the Internet, the Internet activity can be a useful way to expand on the information and vocabulary in the text.

General Suggestions

1. The sequence of readings in this book follows the solar calendar. Although the introductory reading is a good place to begin working with the book, you may want to begin with the holiday that is most imminent, or you may want to ask your students to choose readings which interest them.

2. Divide the class into three groups. Each group does only one of the readings. Then each group explains its passage to the other two groups, putting the key words on the board as it explains.

3. Prepare a double set of 3x5 index cards. Each key word is written on two different cards. For each selection there are 10 different words. Shuffle the 20 cards well and write the numbers 1-20 on the back. Place all the cards on the floor with only the numbers showing. Then in turns the students try to locate the matching pairs by calling out two numbers (see "Matched Pairs" in *Index Card Games for ESL*, Pro Lingua Associates).

4. For review, put the key words from several selections on 3x5 index cards. Divide the class into two teams and have a contest to see which team can use the most words correctly in sentences.

5. Supplement the readings with further cultural exploration:

   a. Ask the students to interview Americans and then compare notes.

   b. Use the material appended to this book to teach songs and to provide a focus for discussions.

Derrick Wallace, 12, a member of the U.S. Navy League Cadet Corps, proudly carries the flag in a parade in Philadelphia, Pennsylvania

Credit AP/WWP H Rumph, Jr

   c. Plan appropriate in-class holiday observances, or participate in school or public ceremonies. Alternatively, plan a party or celebration. Have the students invite friends or give the party for children or for senior citizens. Co-host the party with a church or civic group.

   d. Discuss food that is traditional for each holiday. Bring in favorite recipes and menus, and help the students prepare a holiday meal.

6. Students generally enjoy working together in pairs.

Key Word Index

(The number indicates the number of the lesson the word appears in – see Contents p. v)

achieve 2
admit 5
advertise 14
affection 4
ancestor 19
ancient 2
anniversary 20
annual 16
appropriate 18
assassin 3
atone 20

balloon 16
basket 7
benefit 9
blessing 16
bury 15
bystander 6

calendar 1
campaign 14
candidate 14
candle 18
capture 6
carve 13
cater 18
celebrate 1
celebrity 6
cemetery 9
ceremony 15
character 13
charity 18
clergyman 3
coincide 7
collect 13
comfort 12
commemorate 1
companion 4
competition 11
conflict 5
contribution 12
convert 6

convince 12
costume 13
courage 15
creativity 19
crowd 2
crude 12

dawn 20
debate 14
declare 10
decorate 4
dedicated 15
defend 19
descent 6
disabled 9
discrimination 3
display 17
donation 17
duty 14
dyed 7

elaborate 2
elderly 16
elect 5
election 14
embrace 2
enact 15
encourage 12
establish 8
estimate 6
evil 13
exchange 17
expedition 12

faith 16
farewell 19
fast 20
favorite 17
feast 16
feelings 4
festival 4
finance 12

float 2
focus 19
force 10
free 10

gather 20
get rid of 20
get together 8
ghost 13
gift 7
goal 2
grave 9
greeting card 7

harvest 16
heritage 19
hire 11
holy 13
honor 15
humorous 4

ideal 5
independence 5
injustice 3
integrate 3
invitation 18

legal 1
legend 6
lunar 19

major 20
memorial 3
memories 8
merchant 4
message 11
minimum 11
miracle 6
missing 15
monument 15

naturalization 10
navigate 12
needy 9

obey 10
observe 15
occur 20
opportunity 8
organize 10
origin 9
ornaments 17

parade 7
participate 6
patriotic 9
pennant 6
perform 10
persuade 11
portrait 5
prayer 20
present 19
pride 19
privacy 14
proclaim 8
prosperity 2

racial 3
raise 8
rebirth 7
recognize 10
refreshments 18
refuse 5
registration 14
religious 1
remember 15
renewal 7
repentance 20
representation 10
require 11
reserve 18
resolution 2
respect 8
result 14
reward 19
rights 3
role 8

romance 4
route 12

scary 13
segregate 3
service 9
share 17
solution 11
souvenir 18
sparkle 17
spiritual 3
spouse 4
starvation 16
strike 11
superstition 1
survive 16
swear in 10
sweetheart 4
symbol 7

thought 8
tie 12
toast 2
traditional 18
tragedy 9
treat 13
trick 13
twice 19

unanimously 5
union 11
unite 5

vacation 17
value 8
veteran 9
volunteer 17
vote 14

wages 11
wish 18
wreath 16
wrongdoing 5

yearly 7

Other Publications from Pro Lingua

Plays for the Holidays.

Historical and Cultural Celebrations. 13 plays from Labor Day (Peter MaGuire organizes immigrant workers) to Independence Day (Writing the Declaration of Independence in Philadelphia). The *dramatis personae* include Columbus, The Headless Horsemen, Eisenhower, Scrooge, Pocahontas, Rosa Parks, JFK, Washington, Franklin, and more.

Celebrating American Heroes.

The Playbook is a collection of 13 short plays featuring an interesting group of heroes, from the very famous (Lincoln, Washington, Edison) to the less well-known (Dolley Madison, Jonas Salk, John Muir, Cesar Chavez, Harriet Beecher Stowe). The format of the plays is similar to *Plays for the Holidays,* with a few leading characters, a narrator, and a chorus. The **photocopyable Teacher's Guide** includes several pronunciation and vocabulary worksheets. The plays are also available on a **cassette recording.**

Heroes from American History.

An integrated skills content-based **reader** for intermediate ESL. All the heroes in the playbook (above) are featured, as well as Maya Lin, Eleanor Roosevelt, and the "ordinary citizen." There are maps and timelines that bring out the historical context of the times when these heroes lived.

All Around America.

The Time Traveler's Talk Show. The show stops at 18 famous places around the US. Students read the script, which includes a host, a local guide, guests from the past, and callers from the present. Supplemented with an **Activities Workbook** that builds language skills, with emphasis on idiomatic spoken language. All the scripts are also recorded on two **CDs** for listening practice.

Living in the United States.

A brief introduction to the culture of the US. Part One: Basic Survival Information. Part Two: Customs and Values. Part Three: Country Facts.

North American Indian Tales.

48 animal stories collected from tribes across North America, the tales explain how the world came to be as it is (*How Chipmunk Got its Stripes,* etc.) Each story is on a separate card with a colorful illustration by a popular Native American artist.

For information or to order, visit our webstore www.ProLinguaAssociates.com *or call our* Inquiries/Advice Hotline (800) 366-4775. Email: Info@ProLinguaAssociates.com